THIS BOOK SHOULD BE RETURNED ON OR BEFORE THE LATEST
DATE SHOWN TO THE LIBRARY FROM WHICH IT WAS BORROWED

AUTHOR

SHOTTER, D.

CLASS

E2

TITLE

Romans and Britons in North-West England

Romans and Britons
in North-West England

David Shotter

Centre for North-West Regional Studies
University of Lancaster

1993

General Editor: Oliver M. Westall

Carlisle: miniature bust of a personification of
Carlisle, shown wearing a mural crown.

Romans and Britons
in North-West England

David Shotter

Romans and Britons in North-West England

by David Shotter   05766576

This volume is the twenty-seventh in a series published by the Centre for North-West Regional Studies at the University of Lancaster. Details of other titles in the series which are available may be found at the back of this volume.

ISSN 0308–4310

Copyright © David Shotter, 1993

First edition, 1993

Published by the Centre for North-West Regional Studies, University of Lancaster
Designed and typeset by Carnegie Publishing Ltd., 18 Maynard Street, Preston
Printed and bound in the UK by T. Snape & Co. Ltd., Boltons Court, Preston

British Library Cataloguing-in-Publication Data
A CIP catalogue record for this book is available from the British Library

ISBN 0-901800-19-8

Contents

List of Plates and Figures

Acknowledgements

I should like to put on record my gratitude to Peter Lee of Lancaster University Archaeological Unit who prepared all of the text figures; also to Miss Susan Waddington of the Department of History at Lancaster University for the preparation of the manuscript.

The majority of the photographs used are my own, but I am grateful to a number of people for the use of their photographs – Barri Jones (plates 22 and 36), Alan King (plate 73), Timothy Potter (plate 35), and Joe Thompson (plate 13). I also acknowledge the co-operation of Carlisle Archaeological Unit and Lancaster University Archaeological Unit in allowing me to use material from their excavations prior to publication – title-page plate and plates 18, 19 and 71 (Carlisle Archaeological Unit) and plates 5, 55, 61 and 62 (Lancaster University Archaeological Unit). Thanks are also due to the Trustees of the Senhouse Roman Museum for the use of their photographs (plates 38 and 52), and to a number of museums for permission to photograph objects in their collections – Carlisle (plates 53, 59 and 66), Lancaster (plates 15, 27 and 39), Ribchester (plate 54), National Museum of Antiquities at Edinburgh (plate 2) and Brougham Castle Museum (plate 41).

1. Introduction

The physical environment of north-west England presents marked contrasts, which over the years have played a large part in determining patterns of conquest, occupation and settlement. The mountains of the Lake District are bounded on three sides by coastal plain, and separated from the Pennines on the fourth side by the significant communications corridor consisting of the valleys of the rivers Eden and Lune. Initial Roman strategy took account of the difficulty of this terrain by arranging its domination through control of the Eden and Lune valleys, and of the Solway Plain. This was probably enhanced by a readiness to intervene by means of coastal landings of troops based at Chester.

Further south, a broad contrast obtains between the Pennine foothills in the east and the coastal plain in the west. This coastal plain is itself penetrated by the valleys and broad estuaries of the Dee, Mersey, Ribble, Wyre, Lune and Kent rivers, which flow from the hills and facilitate communications inland from the coast. Conquest here consisted primarily of control of these valleys and their interconnection by means of a road running from Chester to Carlisle.

Obviously, the environment determined the nature of settlement – in ways that ranged from the broad shape of agricultural exploitation to matters such as the availability of timber and stone for building and raw materials for craftsmen. Clearly, there were factors which presented conditions different from those obtaining today – the changing nature of the coastline, forest cover, and climate; however, current evidence suggests that in general during the Roman period exploitation of the landscape was at an impressive level, though building on what already existed to the extent that it has become customary to talk less of the 'Roman occupation' but rather the 'Roman interlude'. Research in the Ribble, Lune, Kent and Eden valleys has indicated the deliberate positioning of farms to employ both the arable soils of the valley floors and the grazing potential of the valley sides, as well as to avail themselves of the developing systems of communication. Similarly, the siting of farms on the lower slopes of the Lake District hills enabled both arable and pastoral potential to be exploited. An added incentive to such siting is the fact, demonstrated by pollen analyses, that favourable climatic conditions probably permitted the growing of cereal crops to a greater altitude than would be contemplated today.

Forest clearance, already underway in the pre-Roman period, was obviously accelerated both by the enhanced demand for timber (for building and heating) and by the need for land for agricultural usage. Consequent soil erosion from higher levels will both have impoverished the land at higher altitudes and have improved fertility at lower levels. Such environmental changes, however, will have required an element of control; some forestry management will have been necessary in order to conserve timber supplies. Overall, whilst the Roman presence may have acted as a catalyst to development in some areas, in general it is probably more accurate to say that it thrived because of the economic vibrancy of the region as a whole. Just as was the case further south, exploitation of the northern environment went a long way to providing the means of support for the Roman garrisons of occupation.

From this it comes as no surprise that north-west England contains a wealth of archaeological sites of all periods, from the prehistoric to the modern. The Roman period is no exception: legionary fortresses, auxiliary forts, fortlets, watch-towers and temporary marching-camps provide the evidence of the military occupation by the Romans, whilst civilian life is attested in small towns (*vici*), industrial sites, farmsteads and at least one major urban centre (Carlisle). Connecting such sites was a network of roads, some of whose routes can still be easily traced on the ground.

However, whilst this abundance of sites has long been appreciated – except perhaps for those of an agricultural nature - work on understanding them properly has been relatively slow, since until the 1970s most excavations were restricted in size and scope. Although small-scale trenching *can* produce dramatic, even inspired, results, there is no doubt that the provision of enhanced financial resources in recent years has enabled work to progress faster and to some degree more systematically.

In the last two decades, we have seen large-scale excavations and survey-projects at sites all across the north-west; these have embraced major fort and *vicus* sites such as Chester, Northwich, Manchester, Ribchester, Lancaster, Watercrook, Ambleside, Papcastle, Ravenglass, Low Borrow Bridge, Old Penrith, Brougham, Bowness-on-Solway, Carlisle, Birdoswald and Bewcastle, as well as sites of the Cumberland Coast. Further, Roman sites have been examined which are apparently non-military in nature, such as Wilderspool, Wigan and Walton-le-Dale; so too have a number of rural sites, such as Cross Hill Farm (Penrith) and Maiden Castle-on-Stainmore. Other sites, which are strictly outside the geographical scope of this book – for example, Vindolanda and Housesteads – have yielded results with important implications for the understanding of north-western sites. As well as this, funds (both public and private) have been provided for aerial reconnaissance which has not only told us much about known sites, but also (particularly in the rural context) shown up large quantities of sites whose existence was not previously suspected.

At the same time, a good deal of work has been done on the recorded finds from north-western sites – the inscriptions, pottery, coins and coin-hoards – which has enabled our understanding of the history of the Roman occupation to be refined considerably. Yet it is as well to remember that still only a tiny percentage of the area covered by Roman sites has been sampled, and that we are therefore still in great danger of producing interpretations and hypotheses which future work will show to have been untenable.

Inevitably, since it is threatened sites which attract funding, excavation has to take place not necessarily where we believe that problems will be solved, but where rescue threats exist. Recent excavations at Watercrook demonstrate the risks this may cause: that work was concerned principally with the civilian settlement (*vicus*), for that was where the rescue threat existed. However, we now know enough to realise that it can be dangerous to hypothesise about the chronology of a Roman fort on the basis of evidence which derives from its *vicus*. In other words, until a major internal fort building is stripped, our views on the fort itself remain largely in the field of conjecture.

Thus, although we can assert with confidence that knowledge has advanced considerably in recent years, there are still many fundamental gaps in that knowledge. Most north-western forts still lack a *detailed* chronology, and some even a basic chronology. There are major sites whose nature is still in doubt, such as Wigan and Kirkham; there are areas in which concentrations of finds or simple logic suggest that sites still await discovery – such as Colne and Burnley in east

Lancashire, or the Fylde, or again south Cumbria; in particular, questions are constantly put regarding Fleetwood, Barrow-in-Furness and the Cartmel peninsula.

Again, the place-names of only three Roman sites in the north-west are known for certain – Deva / Chester, Bremetennacum / Ribchester and Luguvallium / Carlisle; this shortcoming detracts from an understanding of both communications and patterns of garrison-disposition (see Appendix IV). We are accumulating knowledge about rural settlement, but it is certain that a large number of relatively ephemeral earth-work sites must have perished in the face of the plough, and with them substantial numbers of temporary marching-camps for the army on campaign. Such earth-work sites tend to survive well only on marginal land, not subject to plough-damage. As to the towns, – so important a feature of Romanised life – Carlisle has yet to yield a plan of a single complete public building, whilst the smaller towns (*vici*) are known only in fragments and pose considerable problems in chronological interpretation. Until we progress further on questions such as these, ignorance will continue to surround the most important question of all – how did Roman and native coalesce into a Romanised social and economic unity – assuming of course that they did?

Thus, whilst this book will attempt as coherent as possible a view of the 'Roman interlude' in north-west England, many of the views expressed here are necessarily hedged around with caution. Hopefully, therefore, this book is at one and the same time a progress-report and an indication of the major questions which are as yet unresolved, and which present serious challenges to the historians and archaeologists of the future.

2. Before the Romans

Too often, the prehistory of north-west England has been dismissed with inadequate and inaccurate judgements: backward and sparsely populated are descriptions which have been frequently applied.[1] However, the gradual accumulation of evidence and the development of ideas based upon that evidence have begun to reveal a rather different picture. For example, the fact that the products of the Langdale axe factories have been recognised in Europe offers a glimpse of the importance and sophistication of north-western craft and commerce in prehistory. Further, it is a significant shift in perception that has led to historians ceasing to regard the Roman conquest as representing dramatic cultural change in the north-west, but instead applying to it terms such as the 'Roman interlude', signifying that the Roman presence was but an episode in a longer continuum.

As in other parts of Britain, the historian is of course faced with the complete absence of documentation contemporary with the pre-Roman period. Thus, an understanding of the political, social and economic imperatives of the north-west before the coming of the Romans has to be based to a considerable extent on the observations of Roman writers. How far they understood or even cared about the political geography of north-western England has to be open to considerable doubt. Our chief source is the Roman historian, Cornelius Tacitus,[2] a senator of the late first century AD, who in his later years turned to writing: of course, the major reason for his interest in Britain was the fact that his father-in-law, Cnaeus Julius Agricola, was governor of the province between AD 78 and 84, and responsible for the formal annexation of northern Britain to the province. Although we might in these circumstances have expected Tacitus to have been well-informed, there is little evidence to suggest that he delved any more deeply into British culture and society than had earlier writers.[3]

As we shall see in chapter 3, Tacitus tells us that the Brigantes of northern England – the name means 'upland people' – constituted the most populous tribe in Britain; and presumably on the basis of Agricola's campaign in the north-west Tacitus knew of two dominant geographical features – estuaries and woods. However, his lack of real interest is demonstrated by the fact that at one stage he referred to Boudica as queen of the Brigantes. Elsewhere, Tacitus provides some information on political tensions amongst the Brigantes in his account of the quarrels between the queen, Cartimandua, and her husband, Venutius. Further, Tacitus implies tension between different groups in his description of Agricola's tactic of playing groups off against each other (see Appendix I). Some substance is given to these rivalries by the fact that when the north was Romanised, the centre of the *civitas* (Romanised tribe) of the Brigantes lay at Aldborough in Yorkshire; third-century inscriptions indicate the existence of a *civitas* of the Carvetii in the north-west, and the Alexandrian geographer, Ptolemy, writing in the second century AD, mentions the Setantii, who are commonly placed in the Fylde, but who could, it has been suggested, have occupied territory in south Cumbria.[4] Although, therefore, our evidence is lacking in precision, it does strongly suggest the existence of a number of different tribal influences or 'power blocs' in the north.

Plate 1. The hill-fort on Warton Crag, Carnforth.

The policy of Rome towards these northern groups will be explored in the next chapter, but does archaeological evidence offer any clues to the political geography of the north-west which the Romans will have faced?

In early prehistory, sites had been largely undefended; the development of enclosures – whether by ditches, stone walls or wooden palisades – suggests the emergence of new imperatives. Clearly, a dominant requirement was now the ability to protect ones livelihood from marauders – animal or human. Agricultural exploitation was developing in later prehistory, so that lowland areas were extensively farmed in arable and pastoral contexts and upland areas were devoted to the grazing of cattle and of sheep too where there was security from such natural predators as wolves. By such exploitation, farmers might manage to hold their own at a subsistence level, or might assert leadership through their ability to produce a surplus which could be traded.

The development of a society classified on economic grounds clearly led to rivalries within small 'tribal' groups, and in a broader territorial sense between separate groups which could be regarded as separate tribes. Seats of power can be recognised in the appearance of hillforts, although the lack of research as yet hampers an ability to relate all of these sites chronologically; nor is it clear how far these hillforts may have represented places of retreat in time of danger or sites of permanent habitation. Some were small with a single ditch for defence, whilst others were defended by a prominent position and by more complex defence systems. Such 'hierarchies' may point to a growingly complex socio-political structure within these groups.

In the north of the region is a group of hillforts, of which the most significant is Carrock Fell, whilst another group of sites is found in southern Cumbria such as Castle Head, Skelmore Heads and the multivallate

Warton Crag. There are major sites in the Pennines, such as the impressive Almondbury and Ingleborough, the latter sometimes canvassed as the elusive seat of Cartimandua. Further sites can be seen in Cheshire. These may between them represent centres of groups which exercised a major element of independence, but which owed an ultimate allegiance to Cartimandua.

Such developments were themselves catalysts to new requirements; competitiveness will have led to the need to clear more land for cultivation and to acquire the tools with which to manage this. The point has been emphasised by the recognition – for example, at Carlisle – of signs of ploughed fields beneath some Roman military sites. Although it is not clear how far the north-west's deposits of iron ore were exploited in prehistory, clearly the metal-worker emerged as a major figure in later prehistory. The tribal warrior leaders required weaponry and decorative metal-work befitting their status; they also needed to be able to fit out their horses, for, then as now, the ability to ride rather than walk was a sign of status. Just as the metal-worker produced the trappings of that status, so too he manufactured the tools necessary to acquire position in society.

Although the north-west has produced no evidence of coin-use in later prehistory, the acceleration of the production of tools, utensils and decorative objects in metal, stone, wood and pottery should leave us in no doubt that the commercial pace of life was increasing. Similarly such developments also demonstrate the emergence of techniques for the management and transportation of the necessary raw materials.

Thus, when the Romans arrived in north-west England, they will have discovered an area that had been farmed for many hundreds of years. Although some extensive forest-cover remained, that landscape will have been predominantly one of farms and fields, of trackways which gave access to fields and summer-grazing and linked neighbouring sites.

Similarly, the process of the development of hierarchies had probably already led to the identification of tribes or 'sub-groups' other than the Brigantes themselves. Such a growing complexity of political relationships could of course lead to confusion as the Romans tried to come to terms with such difficulties; ultimately, it seems, it provided that common catalyst to Roman success which is summed up in the instruction – 'Divide and Rule'.

Notes

In these footnotes modern authorities will be referred to in an abbreviated form – for example, 'Higham, 1986' – which will be expanded to a full reference in the bibliography. The 'anonymous' citations of the periodicals, *Journal of Roman Studies* (*JRS*) and *Britannia*, refer to the annual summaries of recent work, 'Roman Britain in 19..'.

Footnotes – Chapter 2

1. For the clearest, recent accounts of the prehistory of the north-west, see Higham, 1986, 117–49 and Clare, 1988, 9–27.
2. The most expansive of Tacitus' accounts of Britain is to be found in his *Life of Agricola*; other important passages are to be found in both his *Histories* and his *Annals*. These are all readily accessible in translation in the Penguin Classics series – the *Life of Agricola* by H. Mattingly, the *Histories* by K. Wellesley and the *Annals* by M. Grant.
3. Such as Julius Caesar and Livy.
4. Higham, 1986, 147.

3. The Conquest of North-West England

The Roman conquest of Britain began in AD 43 under the emperor Claudius; by AD 59, the tribes of the south and the Midlands had been brought under control, and together with much of Wales formed the province of Britannia. In that year, the governor, Suetonius Paulinus, was embarking upon what he expected would be the final onslaught against the druidic centres on Anglesey, when he was stopped in his tracks by the rebellion of Boudica, queen of the Iceni. This rebellion was in large measure due to mismanagement by certain Roman officials, and highlighted the need to consolidate what had already been won.

The rebellion also threw into high relief the value of the treaty which the authorities had with Cartimandua, queen of the Brigantes. The existence of this treaty meant that Rome had little immediately to fear from the Brigantes, and Cartimandua early on gave evidence of her good faith by refusing to harbour the Catuvellaunian chieftain, Caratacus. After his original defeat by the armies of Claudius on the Medway, he had retreated through southern England and Wales, hoping that eventually victory would be his. The failure of this 'plan' finally brought him (vainly) to seek Cartimandua's protection. At the same time, however, the rebellion of the Iceni posed a warning of the potential fragility of such treaties as Rome enjoyed with Cartimandua.

As we have seen, the tribal territory of the Brigantes stretched from the north midlands into southern Scotland, excluding only the coastal strip of east Yorkshire, which belonged to the Parisi, a tribe whose cultural links were closest with the Iceni and Coritani further south. The precise tribal boundaries are not known, through the discovery in Dumfriesshire of a relief-carving of the Romanised tutelary deity, *Brigantia*, may indicate their northward extent; indeed the positions of the so-called 'outpost forts' of Hadrian's Wall (Birrens, Netherby and Bewcastle) may be related to the pre-Roman borders of the tribe.

We have observed that culturally the Brigantes were a Bronze Age people, made up of arable farmers, pastoralists, horsebreeders and metal-workers. Their rulers were probably intrusive with affinities further south; the great bank and ditch structures at Stanwick (north Yorkshire), which eventually enclosed around 750 acres, are reminiscent of the enclosed areas of the Catuvellauni in the south, which Julius Caesar had referred to as *oppida*.

The passages of Tacitus (See Appendix I) which refer to Brigantian politics are far from clear in their meaning, and they have generated a considerable literature in recent years.[1] It is clear that Rome entered into some kind of alliance with a Brigantian queen / princess, named Cartimandua. It is not clear when this happened, but it might have been soon after the Claudian invasion in AD 43; for not only did the Romans not apparently have to worry about their northern flank as they turned towards Wales, but, as we have seen, the queen decided not to harbour the Catuvellaunian chieftain, Caratacus, when he sought refuge with her, but preferred (and presumably felt sufficiently strong) to hand him over to Rome.

In Roman eyes, her stature gained from this, as did her wealth and influence. What is

Figure 1. Find-spots of pre-Neronian *Aes* Coins.

Plate 3. Copies of coins of Claudius; the coin on the right was found in Barrow.

Plate 2. Relief of the Romanised deity, Brigantia (National Museum of Antiquities, Edinburgh). The relief, which shows the goddess as a 'winged victory', came from Birrens.

less clear is the course of her relationship with Venutius, her husband at one stage, and described by Tacitus as second only to Caratacus as a warlord. It is evident that although Venutius was anti-Roman by disposition he was kept loyal to Rome so long as he was married to Cartimandua. We may assume therefore that in terms of Brigantian politics the virtue of the marriage was its effect in binding together factions within the tribe and thus allowing Cartimandua's writ to run throughout the tribal area.

It is evident, however, that the Brigantes had something of a reputation for fractiousness, and that the relationship between Cartimandua and Venutius was a tense one, which may have restricted overt manifestations of Venutius' hostility to Rome, but without ameliorating it in principle. Roman intervention in Brigantia was evidently necessary under at least two early governors – Didius Gallus (AD 52–7) and Vettius Bolanus (AD 69–71), although we should note the contrasting views on Bolanus of Tacitus who regards him as inactive, and the late first-century Roman poet, Statius, who implies fierce action during Bolanus' governorship.[2] Further, although this intervention persuaded Venutius to bide his time, it was certainly not easy action for Roman troops.

At some stage the relationship between the two Britons broke down, though it is hard on the basis of Tacitus' evidence to determine precisely when this happened. It would, however, not be unreasonable to suppose that it occurred around AD 57, and that it introduced into Brigantian politics a period of considerable uncertainty. There is no need to assume any kind of reconciliation between Cartimandua and Venutius after AD 57; indeed her marriage to her former husband's armourbearer, Vellocatus, at some point between AD 57 and 69 argues strongly against it.

These events had the effect of turning the client-kingdom into an unstable and potentially hostile neighbour. Skirmishing between the factions of Venutius and Cartimandua is

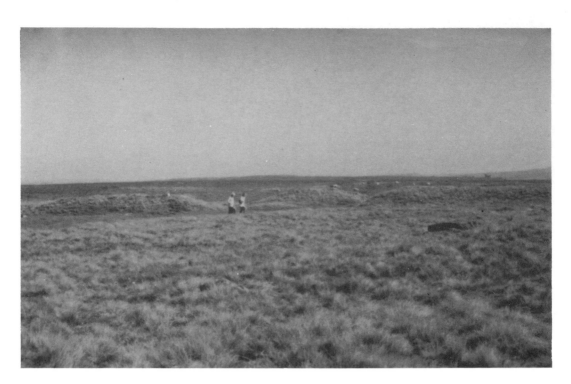

Plate 4. Rey Cross marching-camp: rampart and entrance, seen from the interior.

explicitly confirmed by Tacitus, and this could well have continued over several years and included both 'civil' strife, manoeuvres such as the kidnapping of Venutius' relations, and the introduction of external forces in support of Venutius. These were contexts in which it would have been appropriate to introduce Roman arms; although Tacitus' accounts are, as often, aggravatingly vague in terms of topography and chronology, it is clear that more than one Roman engagement was involved. These disturbances culminated in Venutius taking advantage of the Roman civil war in AD 69 and putting so much pressure on Cartimandua that the Roman forces could do no more than rescue her, leaving Venutius in control of the tribe and thus from the Roman point of view a potentially dangerous situation which would require urgent action as soon as circumstances allowed.

The locations of their respective seats of power are hard to pinpoint: various hillforts, such as Ingleborough and Almondbury, have been canvassed for Cartimandua, though, as we have seen, the most recent evidence from Almondbury would appear to place the period of its use well prior these events. Sir Ian Richmond[3] plausibly suggested that Cartimandua's ability to rule the tribe may have been based upon the wealth and power which were represented by the richly fertile land of the Vale of York: both York itself, whose name (Eboracum) is not of Roman origin, and Aldborough (the later Romanised tribal centre) have been proposed, but both have failed to produce the appropriate pre-Roman evidence. It has been suggested[4] more recently that Stanwick, which has frequently been proposed as Venutius' centre, may in fact have belonged to Cartimandua. The volume of Roman material present on the site, it is argued, is inconsistent with a centre which belonged to Rome's chief adversary in the

Plate 5. Timber rampart-base at Ribchester.

Plate 6. Milestone at Middleton-in Lonsdale. The Roman inscription, MP LIII, indicates a distance of 53 miles, presumably from Carlisle.

region, though it may be suggested that in the fighting in AD 69 Venutius took the site, enlarged it and made it the centre from which he mounted his final resistance to the Roman advance under Petilius Cerialis after AD 71. If these arguments are reasonable, it would not be unsuitable to locate his original centre in or to the west of the Pennines, particularly since much of the albeit tentative evidence for Roman military activity in the pre-Flavian period is located in and to the west of the Pennines. Further, the help which Venutius was able to summon from outside may in this case have come from north Wales, which had still not been properly subdued.

It is usually assumed that the forts at Templeborough (near Rotherham),[5] Chesterfield and possibly Whitchurch date from the 60s, as do those which separate the Brigantes from the Parisi, their neighbours in east Yorkshire. How far this pre-Flavian activity extended west of the Pennines is harder to say; finds of copies of coins of the emperor Claudius, which were circulating in the late 50s and 60s, appear at places along the coast of north-west England from the Dee to the Solway (fig. 1).[6] Whilst as yet there is no *structural* evidence of Roman activity north of Chester during the 60s, these coin-finds suggest that troops may have been shipped from the Dee estuary along the north-west coast in order to effect temporary intervention in local troublespots. The major river estuaries are amongst the likely locations for such activity, and Walton-le-Dale (on the Ribble) has produced at least three coins of the relevant type. One has also been located at Barrow-in-Furness, where firm signs of Roman occupation remain elusive.

11

Plate 7. Flavian-period coins from Carlisle.

Plate 8. *Lilia*-pits at Rough Castle, on the Antonine Wall.

The fate of Cartimandua following her rescue by Roman troops in AD 69 cannot be determined, as there is no subsequent mention of her. Suggestions, however, that she was housed in privileged conditions in Chester are based on evidence which cannot be said to support such a case.

Full conquest of north-west England was left to the Flavian period, following the final collapse of the client-kingdom in AD 69. In particular two governors – Quintus Petilius Cerialis (AD 71–4) and Cnaeus Julius Agricola (AD 78–84)[7] carried the limit of conquered territory from the Dee / Humber line to the Moray Firth. As Tacitus describes it, Cerialis' activity was largely suited to the immediate needs rather than to a permanent occupation. 'After a series of battles, some not uncostly, Petilius had operated, if not actually triumphed, over the major part of their [i.e. the Brigantes'] territory'. The method, though not precisely described by Tacitus, may perhaps be inferred from an earlier comment about this period[8] when Agricola was commander of Legion XX *Valeria Victrix* during Cerialis' governorship. It appears that the forces were split up, and that therefore in all likelihood Cerialis operated on the eastern side of the Pennines with his old legion, Legion IX *Hispana*, whilst Agricola operated in the west. It is usually assumed that during these operations the fortress of Legion IX was advanced from Lincoln to York, and that Cerialis actually defeated Venutius at Stanwick, and linked up with Agricola by crossing the Stainmore Pass.

Traditionally it has been very difficult to find archaeological evidence which can satisfactorily distinguish between sites which belong to the period of Cerialis' governorship and those of Agricolan origin. However, in recent years dates acquired by the technique of dendrochronology have permitted a far greater precision to be achieved. It is likely, because of their relationship with the road, that the temporary marching-camps across Stainmore, such as Rey Cross and Cracken-

Plate 9. Roman road between Ribchester and Burrow-in-Lonsdale (seen from Jeffry Hill).

thorpe, were established by Cerialis.[9] The use of this route in the early Flavian period receives strong confirmation from recent dates established for timbers from the rampart base of the earliest fort at Carlisle; these dates show that the timbers were felled at some stage during the winter of AD 71–2.[10] Confirmation of this date may be found in a significant group of pre-Flavian and early Flavian coins.

Other sites in the north-west belonging to Cerialis' governorship remain hard to locate: it is clear that the auxiliary fort at Chester was manned, and that the process of converting it into a legionary fortress of 55 acres to replace Wroxeter may already have started. It is likely too that Whitchurch and Middlewich were occupied at this time. Artefactual evidence would suggest that Walton-le-Dale should be

Plate 10. Roman road to the south of Low Barrow Bridge.

Plate 11. Circular earthwork on Stainmore: remains of a signal-tower.

included in this group; indeed it is not impossible that the early 70s saw an early fort at Walton-le-Dale being closed down in favour of Ribchester,[11] since the most recent excavations at that site (1989–90) have revealed a complex stratigraphic sequence which is persuasive of military occupation earlier than Agricola's governorship.

Tacitus tells us that during Cerialis' period of office, Agricola, who was then commander of Legion XX, operated independently. It is possible that his brief was to attack western Brigantia from the sea perhaps linking up with Cerialis in Carlisle. In this case, therefore, the early Flavian period saw some activity in the north of Cumbria – perhaps to separate the good agricultural land of the Solway Plain from the hillier country to the south; the recently discovered fort at Blennerhasset (between Old Carlisle and Papcastle) has yielded an assemblage of pottery which is characteristic of occupation in the late Neronian / early Flavian periods.[12]

Blennerhasset, at 8.4 acres, is one of the largest forts in Cumbria, and it is possible that another large fort to the south of Burgh-by-Sands which has been seen from the air, situated close by the recently excavated western Stanegate fort (Burgh I), should find a place in this early period. Further, aerial photographs of Maryport suggest the possibility of a large fort-like structure partially underlying the known fort, which is itself probably of late Flavian date.

The truth, however, of Tacitus' statement concerning the wide-ranging and bloody nature of Cerialis' activities, and with it by implication their thoroughness and effectiveness, is borne out by two considerations. First, it is evident that Cerialis' successor, Julius Frontinus, was able to operate in north Wales with no fear of being 'stabbed in the back': and secondly, there is the fact that when, after the completion of the Welsh conquest, Agricola turned back to the north, he secured it in a single campaigning season.

Tacitus' account of Agricola's campaign against the Brigantes[13] is unsatisfactory in the extreme if we wish to use it to determine Agricola's precise routes. A number of 'shadowy clues' may, however, be put to work; first, it is evident that the campaign represented a twin advance on both sides of the Pennines – a point which has received some corroboration from the discovery in 1974 of a major Agricolan military site at Red House, near Corbridge.[14] Secondly, Tacitus seems to show that Agricola (perhaps reiterating Cerialis' policy) gained the co-operation of the various Brigantian groups by encircling them and thus separating and protecting them from their neighbours. This in its turn would suggest a concentration on the chief river-valleys, which effectively separated the defended sites on the high ground. Detail is of course lacking in our knowledge of this, since whilst we can show a considerable number of hill-forts, few have been examined with a view to establishing whether or not their dating will tie them into this period. Thirdly, a general indication of topography is contained in Tacitus' remark about estuaries and woods, which applies very well to Lancashire in particular. Fourthly, we may infer from this, and from a remark which Tacitus makes about the joint use of fleet and troops in the later Scottish campaigns, that it was Agricola's policy to disembark troops in the main estuaries and march them up the valleys where they could join with troops taking overland routes. Although speculative in the absence of hard evidence, it might be that the site at Kirkham (whose nature and dating are not certain) started in this way and also for that matter a site which may originally have lain at the mouth of the Wyre, and which many have taken to be Ptolemy's elusive *Portus Setantiorum*.

By stressing Agricola's 'omni-presence', Tacitus has in a sense initiated another area of confusion – namely, he appears to have led scholars to think that every known site in north-west England (whatever its nature) is Agricolan; as Professor Barri Jones wrote

Figure 2. Early Flavian sites.

Plate 12. Paved road over Blackstone Edge, Rochdale.

some years ago: ' "Agricolan" is an over-worked adjective'. Fortunately there are ways in which we can distinguish Agricolan from later activity: first, there are some significant differences in the ceramic and numismatic evidence;[15] secondly, by trying to understand Agricola's strategy we can go some way towards working out where we should expect him to have been active. Unfortunately, the most direct form of evidence – that of inscriptions – helps us very little; Agricola's permanent forts, built as they were of turf and timber, will have had *wooden* dedicatory inscriptions, which stand much less chance of survival than their stone equivalents. In fact, apart from the very fragmentary *Basilica*-inscription from Verulamium (St Alban's), only one other 'inscription' bears Agricola's name – on a length of lead water-piping from Chester, dated to AD 79.

A further problem in tracing Agricola's

Plate 13. Roman weapon-heads from Watercrook.

movements is that much of our evidence derives from sites which became permanent, and which therefore provide us with information about the long-term policing network for the area. Some of these may lack occupation from the Agricolan period because Agricolan sites were located near them rather than always providing the earliest levels on such sites of long-term occupation. It is possible in any case that some of the movements of the early Flavian period – or even earlier – were represented only by temporary marching-camps. Because such sites were by their nature occupied only for short periods, they leave little occupation-debris for dating; further, as earth-work sites, they are likely to have been substantially destroyed in areas subject to long-term ploughing, and are therefore identifiable only by the most sophisticated survey-methods. Only when located on land of marginal agricultural value do such sites survive in visible form – as at Rey Cross (Stainmore), Mastiles Lane (Malham Moor), Brackenrigg and Troutbeck.[16] It is virtually impossible to place such sites into a specific model of conquest, though we have seen that there is some reason to place the Stainmore sequence of camps earlier than Agricola's governorship, even though we cannot regard this case as *proved*. It is further worth noting than none of the temporary camps so far identified in north-west England have entrance-ways which conform typologically with the distinctive Agricolan camps located in Scotland at such sites as Stracathro.[17]

We have noted that Agricola's *permanent* forts contained timber buildings and were defended by ramparts of turf and clay laid on a foundation of logs (corduroy). The rampart was often supported by a timber revetment or fence on the inside and sometimes by a complete box-like enclosing fence. Outside were ditches and other obstacles. At Watercrook, for example (itself not an Agricolan site), between the first and second ditch was a palisade fence made probably of branches, and

an earth-and-rubble bank. The rampart was pierced by double-carriageway gates with guard-towers, which led to a central range of buildings consisting of headquarters, granaries and commandant's house, whilst the rest of the area would be occupied largely by barracks and stables.

It should be noted that, whilst it is true that Agricola did not leave stone-built forts, those constructed of turf and timber were chronologically far more widespread than has sometimes been supposed, and therefore do not offer by themselves conclusive evidence of occupation in the Agricolan period.

The obvious base for Agricola's campaign in north-west England was Chester, from where he could advance northwards both by land and sea. It was also a key site for operations in north Wales, where in his first campaigning season Agricola evidently completed the work of his predecessor, Julius Frontinus. The length of lead water-piping, mentioned earlier, which bears Agricola's name and is dated to AD 79, suggests that the conversion of the auxiliary fort to a legionary fortress was probably completed by Agricola. The relevance of Chester to a number of theatres of operation, therefore, suggests that the auxiliary fort on the site which preceded the legionary fortress may have been in place early enough to service the ill-fated attempt of Suetonius Paulinus to subdue north Wales in the late 50s. The conversion to a legionary fortress, whilst clearly a process belonging to the early Flavian period, perhaps makes most sense in the context of the Welsh campaigns of Julius Frontinus.

The direction and extent of Agricola's single campaign in north-west England has always been a matter of considerable speculation. However, the speed of it suggests that much successful work had been achieved by his predecessors, and Tacitus' account indicates that Agricola was able to play 'sub-groups' of the north-western Brigantes off against each other; the removal of both Cartimandua and Venutius had evidently

Plate 14. Lancaster: turf-and-clay rampart.

destroyed the coherence of the tribe. It seems unlikely that Agricola will have had time (and presumably did not need) to do more than to sweep northwards from Chester to Carlisle along a route which later came to represent the chief communications-artery through north-west England. This led along the foot-hills of the Pennines and then followed the lines of the rivers Lune and Eden. Control of these valleys and of the natural passes across the Pennines will have given Agricola an effective stranglehold on the region. It appears that for the time being at least the Lake District could be left largely unattended, and that it was not fully penetrated until later in the first and early in the second centuries AD.

Considerable stretches of the main northward route survive in various forms; between Penrith and Carlisle, the modern A6 follows its route, whilst it can be picked out by minor roads between Manchester and Ribchester, between Ribchester and Burrow-in-Lonsdale, and a particularly impressive stretch can be seen from Jeffry Hill (on Longridge Fell) as the road heads northwards to cross the river Hodder.[18] Further north, stretches of minor road reflect the original course near Burrow-in-Lonsdale, and a cylin-drical stone now functioning as a parish boundary may be the surviving stump of an *in situ* milestone. South of Low Borrow Bridge, the road is impressively preserved on the eastern side of the Lune Valley, and a recent (1991) excavation at Orton has revealed its construction with a distinctive central spine of heavy cobbles. The road also survives in part as an earthwork in Barbondale, with a complete milestone surviving at Middleton-in-Lonsdale, although not standing precisely at its original location.

Agricola's northward advance started at Chester; excavations over the years have

Plate 15. Hadrianic milestone from Caton (Lancaster City Museum and Art Gallery). The inscription reads: 'For the Emperor Caesar Trajan Hadrian Augustus, Chief Priest, with Tribunician Power, three times Consul, Father of his Country, from . . . 4 miles.'

revealed buildings of many periods both inside and outside the legionary fortress.[19] Those of 1978 on Abbey Green, however, demonstrated the existence of a turf rampart which clearly represents the primary phase of the fortress-defences. From Chester, the route led to Northwich,[20] the intermediate point between Chester and Manchester; work in the late 1960s revealed elements of a turf-and-timber fort of the Flavian period on Castle Hill. This has subsequently been shown to have been partly overlain by another fort, probably of second-century date.

Excavation and observation over the years has established the layout of an auxiliary fort at Manchester on Castlefield (off Deans-gate).[21] Recent excavations on the northern and western defences[22] have shown elements of the northern gateway, rampart and ditch-system of a fort which evidently had two turf-and-timber phases, the earlier of which is regarded as of Agricolan date, the second late Flavian / Trajanic: the fort was evidently substantially enlarged around the middle of the second century, perhaps following the withdrawal from the Antonine Wall in *c*. AD 165. It is worth noting that outside the western ditches lay pits interpreted as a defensive feature known as *lilia*; a sharpened stake was inserted into each pit, with its point up-turned, and the pit then covered with brushwood to provide an extremely hazardous 'man-trap'. A very fine example of this feature is to be seen to the north of the Antonine Wall, at Rough Castle.

North of Manchester, the situation becomes more complex; although a road runs northwards via Affetside to Ribchester, the third-century road-list, known as *The Antonine Itinerary*, indicates a route from Ribchester to Manchester which has an intermediate site, named Coccium. This has usually been taken to be Wigan,[23] where many Roman finds have been made, and where in recent years excavations have revealed timber buildings with three phrases of occupation, which have been placed between the early second and early third centuries. There is nothing in the present evidence to suggest either that these structures were of military origin or that they played any part in the original conquest of the north-west. If Coccium is indeed Wigan (and not another site between Manchester and Ribchester), then we should regard the route given in *The Antonine Itinerary* as of later significance when consolidation of the original conquest had resulted in a greater complexity of site-distribution (see below in chapter 4).

At Ribchester, the evidence points to a foundation at least as early as Agricola's governorship, and recent work (1989–90) in the area of the extended church graveyard has indicated complexity in the earlier phases of occupation and that the origin of the site may go back to the period of Cerialis. A good deal of the fort's area – approximately 30 per cent – has been lost to erosion by the river, but what remains provides evidence of fort-phases both of turf-and-timber construction and of stone-building. The excavated remains probably indicate re-orientation or realignment of the fort at some stage – perhaps during the second century AD - and this may be connected with a garrison-change; the early garrison of Asturian cavalry from Spain was probably redeployed on Hadrian's Wall early in the second century AD, and later in that century Ribchester received a part of the large group of Sarmatian cavalry brought from the Danube by the emperor, Marcus Aurelius (AD 161–80).

Elements of the defences of the Ribchester forts have been observed in a number of recent excavations – a clay-and-turf rampart rested on a log-base (known as a corduroy), and at one point it could be seen that the turves were approximately one foot square, and that each layer was interleaved with brushwood. The multi-phase ditches include three different types – a traditional V-shaped ditch, a 'Punic' ditch (with a near-vertical outer face), and a much shallower type which can still be seen as feature in some of the fields near to the church.

As well as being placed on the north-south road, Ribchester lay on a road which ran along the north bank of the Ribble; this road ran to the north of Preston to Kirkham,[24] and may then have turned north to the mouth of the river Wyre, perhaps terminating at a site which has possibly been lost off the coast near Fleetwood. It has long been held that this site may have been Ptolemy's *Portus Setantiorum*, and that the Setantii were a sub-group of the Brigantes, living in or close to the Fylde.

South of the Ribble at its confluence with the Darwen, lies Walton-le-Dale. Speculation about this site has been intense in the past, but recent excavations appear to have put beyond reasonable doubt the likelihood that the site was military in nature.[25] On the other hand, it has to be said that the buildings excavated do not resemble those of a conventional fort layout. Though of a large scale they would appear to be more consistent with a manu-facture, storage and supply role.

A possibility, which remains to be fully considered, is that these buildings may have been preceded by a conventional fort dating back as early as the 60s and relating to the earliest intervention in the area; the river Ribble will have provided an excellent line for penetration and communication. This pre-sumed early site at Walton-le-Dale would appear to have been abandoned by the early 70s, and the storage buildings were constructed only after an interval of inactivity at the site.

From both Ribchester and Manchester run trans-Pennine links: from Manchester a road runs across Saddleworth Moor, heading for York; there are forts along it at Castleshaw and Slack. At the former, there is a large fort, which has timber buildings and which has been assumed to be Agricolan, and a smaller later fort inside[26] and partly contiguous with it. This later fortlet, which is assumed to have been Trajanic in date contained a rather strange collection of buildings consisting of a barrack-block, a courtyard building, a com-mander's house (with a bath-house), latrines and a granary which was apparently larger than this fortlet would require. Both fort and fortlet, each of which probably had two phases of construction, were contained within turf ramparts.

Another road heads from Manchester to Ilkley, though doubt continues to surround the relation to it of the paved surface which runs over Blackstone Edge; yet another leads south-eastwards towards Melandra[27] and Brough-on-Noe.[28] It is likely that the Ribble–Aire corridor[29] was supplied with a signalling system similar to that identified over Stainmore (see below). Indeed the existence of a small earthwork at Mellor Hill, above Ribchester, may be a fragment of it. It is further possible that a site of a similar nature may await discovery near Whalley, to judge from occasional finds of Roman material in the area, and the presence of an altar (probably to the god, Mars) in Whalley church[30] – that is, if this has not been transported from elsewhere.

The military road ran northwards from Ribchester to Burrow-in-Lonsdale:[31] the road itself is still impressively preserved over a number of stretches, although of the fort at Burrow virtually nothing can be seen. The fort, like many, is protected by a confluence of rivers – in this case, the Lune and the Leck Beck; it lies at a distance from the main north–south route which prompts the suggestion that it may not be the earliest military site in the area. Limited excavation has taken place, but on the whole tells us more of the later stages of the fort's development than of its initial phases, although it appears that at some stage re-orientation occurred. A turf-and-timber phase was located and, although not certainly dated, it would not be inconsistent with an Agricolan beginning.

If that is so, then we can see Burrow as occupying a crucial position in the Lune valley control-system, since it looks in one direction to Low Borrow Bridge in the upper Lune gorge and in the other to Lancaster up to which point at least the river Lune was navigable.

The fort site at Lancaster occupies, rather unusually, a hill-top position. Although it is clear that the sequence of structures, military and civilian, on Castle Hill is complex, we can now be virtually certain of an Agricolan beginning, both on ceramic and numismatic evidence.[32] In the grounds of the old vicarage, running east-west, was an especially well-preserved turf-and-clay rampart, surviving to a height of 1.3 metres. Since this rampart had timber buildings erected across it, we can only assume that later forts were larger, and that the rampart survived because the whole platform had been levelled up. Further, there was no sign of the Trajanic stone rampart to be inferred from a building-slab found in the Priory Church.[33] However, the discovery of a bevelled plinth course on a line that would take it only a few yards north of the clay-and-turf rampart suggests that on the north side at least the enlargement was not great. If this was the northern defence of the Agricolan fort, it is likely that the western defence of the same fort was located in western Vicarage Field in 1971. On the other hand, although an eastern gateway was found near the junction of Church Street and China Street, there was no evidence there of a turf-and-timber phase, suggesting that the eastern rampart of the Agricolan fort was a little higher up Castle Hill. It is also worth noting that at some stage before it went out of use, this turf rampart underwent a modification, possibly indicating a short break in occupation in the later Flavian period – a suggestion which would not be at variance with the numismatic record.[34]

A road running on the south bank of the Lune towards Burrow is certainly attested in the Hadrianic period by the fine milestone found at Caton. In addition, stretches of this road were observed in 1992 during pipeline-work in the Quernmore / Caton / Brookhouse area. The Lune valley route joined the Ribchester–Burrow road possibly at its crossing of the Wenning.[35] The upper Lune was protected by the fort at Low Borrow Bridge (Tebay), the outline of which is still clearly preserved. Excavation of the site has been limited, and the dating evidence, although consistent with pre-Hadrianic activity, does not require a date as early as Agricolan. However, it does not seem reasonable that Agricola did not establish a site in this area: thus, either an Agricolan site awaits location or, rather like Lancaster and as suggested by Hildyard,[36] the Agricolan fort was a smaller one situated within the area of the later fort. The most recent excavations (approximately half a mile south of the fort) have revealed the road running south from the fort and part of the site-cemetery on its eastern side.

At Brougham, the north–south route joined with that coming across Stainmore. As has already been noted, it is usually held that the Stainmore road belongs to the movements of Petilius Cerialis, but that the marching-camps could date to the governorship of either Cerialis or Agricola. Four marching- or campaign-camps are known in the area – Rey Cross, Crackenthorpe, Kirkby Thore and Plumpton Head;[37] such camps were intended for legions on the march, and consisted of a clear, open, space defended by a rampart-bank, possibly crowned by a palisade, and an outer ditch. The space was used for pitching the army's tents. The shapes of these camps are by no means as regular as those of permanent forts: whilst Rey Cross is rectilinear, Plumpton Head forms an irregular trapezoidal shape. The finest of the camps is undeniably Rey Cross, which still has a near-complete rampart-circuit and entrances defended by outer covering mounds (*tutuli*). Recent excavations at Rey Cross have revealed 'post-holes' which may have resulted from the use of tent-pegs. Further, the discovery of some third-century pottery suggests that the site may have had a use other than simply one that related to the initial conquest of the north-west.

In addition, a line of permanent forts crosses the pass – from Greta Bridge through Bowes, Brough and Kirkby Thore to Brougham. Between Bowes and Brough is the much smaller fort of Maiden Castle. Of these, Greta Bridge and Brougham have usually been assumed to have been Agricolan foundations, although there is no proof of this: at Kirkby Thore[38] a turf-and-clay rampart inside the later fort may be Agricolan, and a similar defensive arrangement at Bowes was attributed to Agricola.[39] Brough-under-Stainmore has seen some excavation,[40] though

Plate 16. Low Burrow Bridge: the Roman fort.

23

in the case of this fort, it is the chance finds of coins and pottery that point to an Agricolan foundation rather than anything structural revealed by the excavations themselves. Finally, the fortlet at Maiden Castle, which covers approximately half an acre, may well have been more concerned with a signalling and watching role than employed as a garrison-fort. Finds have been too few to postulate a chronology: the fortlet was equipped with a stone rampart, and whilst occupation from the Flavian period is not ruled out by the finds, a second-century foundation seems more likely.

Alongside the temporary camps and permanent forts across Stainmore, there are also signal- or watch-towers, three on Stainmore itself, if we include Maiden Castle.[41] Bowes Moor and Roper Castle are closely comparable as oblong earthworks. In recent years, it has been shown that there are other small sites on the western approaches to Stainmore in the form of earthworks made up of a 'platform' with a four-post tower protected by two ditches. Sites of this kind observed and part-tested are Punchbowl Inn, Augill Bridge, Appleby Golf Course and Johnson's Plain.[42] However, a similar earth-work at Augill Castle has been tested, and found not to be of this type: this urges caution in the interpretation of such sites. It has been suggested that the close proximity of these sites one to another was due to the fact that visibility in the area was frequently poor. There is at present no conclusive evidence by which to date these 'western Stain-móre' sites, although it is hard to believe that their inception is later than the first century. However, excavation at the rectilinear site at Bowes Moor has produced

Plate 17. Brougham: the medieval castle standing at the north-west corner of the Roman fort, which survives as a 'playing-card' shaped earthwork.

pottery which is mid-fourth century in date. We thus have to exercise great care in assessing the chronological relationships of the Stainmore sites.

As has already been noted, the Stainmore and north–south roads meet at Brougham: the rectangular earthwork of the Roman fort is plainly visible. Whilst there is little dating evidence for the site, it is hardly conceivable that this important road-junction fort does not go back at least to Agricola's period of office.[43]

From Brougham, the main north–south route follows the modern A6 closely. Just north of Penrith lies the fort of Old Penrith: a relatively extensive excavation in 1977–8 produced evidence which suggested that the fort came into operation in the post-Agricolan period, although it must be borne in mind that the excavation was largely concerned with the *vicus* on the south side of the fort, and that it may therefore be premature to infer too much from it about the history of the fort itself.[44] There are at least three other sites in the close vicinity which have been identified from the air. One of these is probably a marching-camp, the other two, though likely military, are of uncertain type. Excavation has suggested that occupation of one of these latter does not begin until the second century.[45]

A number of sites have been located in the vicinity of the road north to Carlisle: at least two marching-camps lie astride the road; also a tilery at Scalesceugh which was producing material from the first to the fourth century.[46] Of the presumed forts, Park House is now regarded as a farmstead,[47] whilst both Wreay Hall and Barrock Fell are almost certainly fortlets of considerably later – probably fourth-century – date.[48]

Despite the large amounts of Roman material collected in Carlisle over the years, it is only since the early 1970s that the city has seen a large and near-continuous excavation-programme. Roman occupation of many periods has been revealed, although the earliest material currently known comes from two sites separated by more than 400 metres – a civilian building at Blackfriars Street and the spectacular remains of turf-and-timber construction in the Annetwell Street / Abbey Street area. The distance between these two early sites indicates the speed at which Roman Carlisle must have developed in its earliest years.

The excavations of Blackfriars Street[49] have revealed that Blackfriars Street is itself on the line of a Roman street of the Flavian period with typical town (*vicus*)-building fronting it – long, narrow, 'strip'-buildings, timber-framed, and with their gable-ends facing on to the street. The same type of building can be seen, although in stone-built form, at Vindolanda, and these particular buildings in Carlisle appear to have remained in use into the late fourth and early fifth centuries (see below in chapter 7).

The site in the Annetwell Street / Abbey Street[50] area has seen a considerable amount of excavation since the early 1970s: it is evident that it is military in nature, and five separate phases of fort-construction have been distinguished. The excavations indicated that the southern elements of the fort-defences lay within their area, whilst the bulk of the fort lay to the north under the area subsequently covered by the medieval castle. The development of the fort clearly involved some enlargement, and began with two phases of turf-and-timber construction (between the Flavian and early Antonine periods), two subsequent phases which began c. AD 165 in which stone buildings were enclosed within turf ramparts, and a final phase in the third century in which the rampart was modified by the addition of a stone wall.

The excavations have been distinguished by the revelation of exceptionally well preserved timbers; dendrochronological tests on these indicate that the inception of the first phase of fort-construction should be placed in the period of Cerialis' governorship (AD 71–2), although building-work continued

Plate 18. Carlisle: timber fort gateway.

into the Agricolan period. The high standard of preservation of organic material allowed a close study to be undertaken of the south gateway, which has two 'carriageways' of timber, one of which had been so deeply rutted by cart-wheels that it had required replacement. The gateway led to a gravelled roadway inside the fort which had been laid on to a corduroy of logs. The excavations also revealed well preserved sections of turf rampart, also laid on a log corduroy, and climbed by a gravelled service-trackway, known as an *ascensus*; the *intervallum*-road (interior service road) was located, as well as elements of barracks. There were also sheds of post-and-wattle construction, some of which may have had a connection with leather -tanning. This later feature may suggest that initially at least the site was more akin to a depot than simply a fort, and might therefore prompt a comparison with the Red House

site, near Corbridge, at the eastern end of the Stanegate road.

Further significant features have been found to the south of the fort: the excavations in Castle Street revealed signs of industrial activity,[51] and the massive timber platform observed beneath the Museum has yet to be explained. It has sometimes been suggested that the Cathedral overlies significant Roman buildings, but the excavations on the site in 1988 concentrated on later Roman levels. As we shall see (below in chapter 6), the important buildings located in the Lanes excavations serve to emphasise the significance of Carlisle; tile-stamps of all of the British legions have been recovered from the city, and one of the Vindolanda documents refers to the presence there of a *centurio regionarius* – a kind of District Commissioner.[52] The same source refers to *Luguvallium*, making Carlisle one of the few sites

Plate 19. Carlisle: timber rampart-base.

in north-west England of which the Roman name is known for certain.

The recently refined dating for the origin of Carlisle has implications also for the understanding of the Stanegate road. Whilst it is clear that the road must be at least as early as Agricola's governorship, it is possible that it could be seen as one of a number of east–west roads for which Cerialis may have been responsible – at least in part. Carlisle and Corbridge were plainly the key sites on the Stanegate, though the dating of other forts and fortlets is less secure than is the case with the principal sites. The chronological problems are further compounded by the recent recognition of the westward extension of the Stanegate from Carlisle to Kirkbride through the newly discovered sites at Burgh-by-Sands and Finglandrigg, which will be considered more fully in the next chapter.[53] There seems little doubt that the sites between Carlisle and

Corbridge, such as Newbrough, Chesterholm (Vindolanda), Carvoran and Brampton Old Church, are a mixture of late Flavian and Trajanic constructions,[54] as are the smaller sites such as Haltwhistle Burn and Throp. Nether Denton, however, may be of Agricolan date.[55]

It is unclear how far Agricola's (or Cerialis') armies may have concerned themselves with the fertile lands of north Cumbria (the Solway Plain), which were to be so important in the second century. As noted above, preliminary assessments of the dating evidence from the recently discovered site at Blennerhasset open up the question afresh. Lying as it does between Carlisle and the coast near the line later formalised through Old Carlisle (Red Dial) and Papcastle to Maryport, the existence of a site at Blennerhasset prompts the suggestion that it may have been part of a line intended to separate the coastal area from the interior. A parallel suggests itself in the early separation of the coastal Parisi of east Yorkshire from their Brigantian neighbours. Indeed it seems possible that the agricultural development of the Solway Plain represented a large measure of the wealth which enabled the Carvetii to be given some autonomy, (based upon the urban centre of Carlisle), in the third century.

Agricola did not intend the Stanegate as a conventional frontier, but perhaps as one of a number of east-west lines (like the Stainmore Pass and the Aire Gap) which served to break up Brigantian territory into segments which could be policed. Agricola's later work was concerned with Scotland, and it was clearly his intention to subdue the whole of the British Isles. Unfortunately for him, Britain could not be viewed in isolation, and by the early 80s it was clear that troops were going to be required to defend more vital territory in Europe. In 83 or 84, Agricola was recalled, and soon after, the Legion II *Adiutrix* was taken from Chester and replaced by the Legion XX *Valeria Victrix*. This in its turn meant the abandonment of Inchtuthil in Perthshire; this still-uncompleted base was vital to the holding of northern Scotland. Thus within two or three years of Agricola's departure Roman arms returned to the line of the Forth and Clyde.

Tacitus saw this as a sell-out; 'Britain was completely conquered, and immediately allowed to slip'. But the decision was a realistic one, viewing the empire as a whole, particularly since there was obviously a good deal of consolidation work to be done in Britain – not least in the Lake District which Agricola had left virtually untouched.[56]

Footnotes – Chapter 3

1. *Life of Agricola* 16–17; *Histories* III.45; *Annals* XII.40. The latter two are set out in full as Appendix I.
2. *Life of Agricola* 8; Statius *Silvae* v.2, 31–47.
3. Richmond, 1954; cf. Hartley, 1980.
4. Hanson 1987, 59–60; Braund, 1984; Hanson and Campbell, 1986; for recent work at Stanwick, see *Britannia* XIII (1982), 348 and XXI (1990), 325.
5. Jones G. D. B., 1968, 2; Jones M. J., 1975, 178.
6. Shotter, 1990, 231.
7. Birley A. R., 1975.
8. *Life of Agricola* 7–8.
9. Birley A. R., 1973, 188f.
10. For a summary, see *Britannia* XXI (1990), 320.
11. For summaries of work carried out at Walton-le-Dale, see *Britannia* XII (1981), 331 and XIII (1982), 352; For the recent work at Ribchester, see *Britannia* XXI (1990), 328.
12. For this site, see Evans and Scull, 1990.
13. *Life of Agricola* 20.
14. Hanson *et al*, 1979.
15. Shotter, 1979, 8; Potter, 1979, 356ff; Breeze, 1988.
16. *Britannia* V (1974), 412 f. (Troutbeck); *Britannia* XVI (1985), 274 (Brackenrigg).
17. Webster, 1970, 172.
18. Graystone, 1992, 13ff.
19. Thompson, 1965, 24ff; Jones M. J., 1975, 142; for further summaries, see *Britannia* VII (1976), 319ff. and VIII (1977), 385ff.
20. Jones G. D. B., 1972; Jones M. J., 1975, 170f. For a summary of recent work at the site, see *Britannia* XV (1984), 288.
21. Bruton, 1909; *JRS* LVI (1966), 200.
22. Jones G. D. B., 1974, 23f; *Britannia* VII (1976), 319; XI (1980), 364; XII (1981), 331; XIII (1982), 352; XVII (1986), 385.
23. *Britannia* XV (1984), 286.
24. Jones M. J., 1975, 159.
25. See *Britannia* XIII (1982), 352.
26. Bruton, 1908; *JRS* LIV (1964), 157; Start, 1985.
27. Jones M. J., 1975, 166f.
28. Jones and Wild, 1970.
29. Jones M. J., 1975, 149.
30. Jones G. D. B., 1970, 3.
31. Birley E. B., 1946; Hildyard, 1954.
32. For work at Lancaster, see Jones and Shotter, 1988 and Shotter and White, 1990.
33. *RIB* 604.
34. Shotter, 1979.
35. Birley E. B., 1946, 145. The Hadrianic date is attested by the milestone found in the Artle Beck at Caton (*RIB* 2272).
36. Birley E. B., 1947; Hildyard, 1951.

37. For Rey Cross and Crackenthorpe, see Richmond and McIntyre, 1934, and *Britannia* XXII (1991), 235f.; for Kirkby Thore, see *Britannia* X (1979), 283; for Plumpton Head, see *Britannia* VI (1975), 232f.
38. For the most recent work, see Gibbons, 1989, particularly p. 108; also Charlesworth, 1964.
39. *JRS* LVII (1968), 179f.
40. Birley E. B., 1958; Jones M. J., 1977.
41. Richmond, 1951.
42. Woolliscroft and Swain, 1991; for the Stainmore sites, see Higham and Jones, 1975.
43. Birley E. B., 1932.
44. Austen, 1991.
45. St. Joseph, 1951; Poulter, 1982.
46. Bellhouse, 1971.
47. Bellhouse, 1954a; Higham and Jones, 1975, 34.
48. Bellhouse, 1953; Collingwood, 1931.
49. McCarthy, 1990.
50. Britannia XXI (1990), 320.
51. McCarthy, 1991.
52. Bowman and Thomas, 1983 (Document no. 22). For a reference on a tablet from Carlisle itself, see *Britannia* XIX (1988), 496.
53. Bellhouse and Richardson, 1982; *Britannia* X (1979), 281ff; Jones G. D. B., 1982, 284f; for Finglandrigg, see *Britannia* XIII (1982), 345 and XV (1984), 281.
54. Breeze and Dobson, 1976, 20ff.
55. Jones M. J., 1975, 169.
56. Hartley, 1966, 12.

4. The Military Consolidation of the North-West

In territorial terms, much of north-west England had been left untouched in the initial conquest; there is no suggestion that in the years following Agricola's departure there was any disturbance to the peace. Clearly, however, the policing network needed to be extended across the area in order to make it effective. There is no real indication concerning the chronological development of consolidation except that it appears to cover the period from AD 90 to 130.

We have very little help from the literary evidence, with the result that two events dominate – the departure of Agricola and the building of Hadrian's Wall almost forty years later; the period between these events is one of the less well-known episodes in Romano–British history. Yet it contains not only the events that led up to the building of Britain's best-known Roman structure, but also the complete withdrawal from Scotland. For this period, therefore, we are more than ever reliant on scraps of literary information, together with the evidence of inscriptions, and the interpretation of numismatic, ceramic and stratigraphic evidence from the sites themselves.

Tacitus published his biography of Agricola in AD 98, two years after the death of the emperor Domitian, about whom the historian was less than enthusiastic; it is clear that he held Domitian as having been maliciously responsible for the fact that Agricola obtained no further post of responsibility after Britain; and there is more than a hint that the emperor may not have been entirely free of having had a hand in Agricola's death in AD 93 at the early age of 53. It is hardly likely, therefore, that Tacitus can be regarded as an entirely unbiased source for the events of Domitian's reign.

At the opening of his *Histories*,[1] five Latin words sum up the Flavian achievement in Britain, as Tacitus saw it: 'Britain was totally conquered, and immediately let slip'. In a sense, we can confirm Tacitus' judgement by noting the situation at Agricola's departure, where the Caledonians had been defeated at *Mons Graupius* in north-east Scotland,[2] and where there seemed no further enemy left – except the terrain: with it we may compare the extremely cryptic reference by Spartianus, the biographer of Hadrian,[3] to the fact that at the time of Trajan's death in the east in AD 117, 'the Britons could not be kept under Roman control'. Between these two dates we know that one of Agricola's successors in Britain, Sallustius Lucullus, was executed allegedly for having named a new type of lance after himself:[4] since this happened in AD 89 it is likely that it was not unconnected with a serious rebellion on the Rhine, instigated by one Antonius Saturninus. Further, the poet Juvenal, in a satire about Domitian's court,[5] mentions hopes of capturing Arviragus of the Britons – obviously a name of some significance to find a place in a work intended for a Roman audience. He also refers in another satire[6] to soldiers 'blooding' themselves in battle with the Brigantes – which must presumably have a 'dramatic date' of *c.* AD 100.

The only other piece of documentary evidence consists of a coin of Hadrian, bearing the legend BRITANNIA[7] – distinct from the BRITANNIA coin issued a little later in the reign to commemorate Hadrian's journey to Britain. The coin was issued in AD 119 – that

Plate 20. Troutbeck: rampart and entrance of marching-camp.

is, during the governorship of Quintus Pompeius Falco, – and must surely refer to victories which were the result of Hadrian's initial response to the problems alluded to by Spartianus.

When Agricola was replaced in AD 83 or 84, the initial imperative was the clarification of the arrangements in the far north – whether the aim of total conquest was to be pursued or whether a territorial compromise would be necessary. Although the building work on Agricola's northern Scottish sites was continued under his successor,[8] by AD 87 a decision appears to have been reached to abandon this work, including that on the legionary fortress at Inchtuthil, and consolidate on the line between the Forth and the Clyde, which had already been recognised as a feasible frontier (*terminus*) and partly fortified by Agricola. Some of the troops released in this way, including Legion II *Adiutrix*, were redeployed on to the mainland of Europe, whilst others were presumably moved to other garrison-points within northern Britain. This was the means by which military consolidation further south was initiated, though our general ignorance regarding the identities of units concerned makes it virtually impossible to plot these movements at all precisely.

In circumstances which are not at all well understood, by c. AD 100 the Forth–Clyde 'frontier' had been abandoned (or lost), the southern Scottish sites deserted, and work in hand on developing the Stanegate road in northern England as the new frontier.

That this was planned too long in advance hardly seems likely in view of the fact that the post-Agriolan period had seen a substantial investment of effort in the forts of lowland Scotland, including a considerable enlargement of the key site of Newstead (in

Roxburghshire). The relinquishing of southern Scotland may have been made inevitable by further troop withdrawals from Britain as the Danube crisis deepened in the later years of Domitian's reign. This in its turn could have precipitated the disturbance in northern Britain at which Juvenal hinted. However, although dating of sites in northern England cannot be precisely achieved, it does appear that work on the 'Stanegate frontier' preceded the loss of lowland Scotland which prompts the suggestion that this work may have been undertaken not after the withdrawal, but in preparation for it.

Such events might seem to corroborate Tacitus' serious misgivings about the situation in Britain in the late Flavian period. Fortunately, however, we have a sufficient body of archaeological data to demonstrate that the period had its positive side also. The late Flavian work on the Stanegate itself shows that it was not intended that the rot should run any deeper. There were apparently two stages to this work – the watch-towers and perhaps the smaller forts, followed by a series of major forts. It is likely that the western extension to the Stanegate should be dated to this period, running from Carlisle through newly recognised sites at Burgh and Finglandrigg to the coast at Kirkbride. At Burgh I (about 1000 metres south of Burgh-by-Sands), two constructional phases were recovered: these consisted of a four-posted watch-tower defended by a circular ditch (reminiscent of the Agricolan towers on the western approaches to Stainmore), superseded by a large auxiliary fort. It appears that the watch-tower was in use for only a short period in the late 90s, whilst the fort was occupied from c. AD 100 to c. AD 125, its demise coinciding with the inception of the fort phase of Hadrian's Wall. The purpose of

Plate 21. Vindolanda: the fort and Stanegate road.

Figure 3. Pre-Hadrianic sites.

such defences on the southern shore of the Solway perhaps reflects the same preoccupation as the coastal extension of Hadrian's Wall (see below in chapter 4) – fear of predatory raids from Galloway which threatened harm to the developing rural economy of the Solway Plain, much as the early Flavian line from Carlisle through Blennerhasset had sought to protect this same area from the south.

At the same time there is clearly still a great deal to be understood about late Flavian / Trajanic frontier arrangements[9] – in particular, the large number of building-phases evident at some of the sites – four, for example, in this period at Corbridge and Chesterholm (Vindolanda).

Thus one, perhaps the major, element of the post-Agricolan consolidation was the provision of a visible frontier to the north of the province. As we have already seen, the Lake District appears to have been the major part of north-west England which Agricola had left untouched. It is largely through critical studies of the pottery and coin-loss evidence that we have come to recognise the sites that are post-Agricolan in date. The chief forts that pierce and surround the Lake District, in addition to those Agricolan and probable Agricolan sites on the Lune and the Eden, are Old Carlisle, Papcastle, Caermote,

Plate 22. Burgh I: four-posted signal-tower, located beneath the Trajanic fort (photograph, G. D. B. Jones).

Old Penrith, Troutbeck, Ambleside, Hardknott, Ravenglass and Watercrook: as well as these there are the coastal forts of Beckfoot, Maryport, Burrow Walls and Moresby, which will be discussed more fully in the next chapter.

Few of these have seen large-scale work; in the north, as we have seen, a road ran from Carlisle in a south-westerly direction through Old Carlisle (Red Dial), Caermote and Papcastle to the coast at Maryport. Old Carlisle,[10] a fort with an extensive and evidently well-preserved *vicus*, is virtually untouched by excavation, and so no chronology can be proposed for the site. Papcastle[11] has seen a large excavation in the mid-1980s on an important *vicus*-building, which has provided evidence of possible military connections with eastern Europe. Earlier work revealed evidence of timber structures and artefactual material which, though not decisive, do not rule out a late Flavian origin.[12] The fact that the fort is larger than many may single it out as having special responsibilities in the north Lakes. At Caermote,[13] two turf-and-timber forts have been found, one inside the other. The larger is the earlier fort, and a Trajanic date for the larger, and a Hadrianic date for the smaller, would not be inconsistent with the evidence. The dating evidence would not appear to support the Agricolan foundation which has been argued on grounds of gateway-style.

On the eastern side of the Lakes, recent excavation at Old Penrith has argued for a date not earlier than the late Flavian period,[14] although it should be remembered that chronological coincidence between fort and *vicus* occupation should not necessarily be assumed. Brougham fort has produced no evidence, though burials in the cemetery were dated to the second and third centuries AD.[15] At Low Borrow Bridge, as we have seen, there is some suggestion of an enlargement of the fort in the form of a pebbly-clay rampart which may have been associated with a stone wall: however, even if the interpretation is

Plate 23. Watercrook: the fort situated in a 'bow' of the river Kent.

correct, dating remains hazardous, although a second-century date for the 'larger' fort cannot be ruled out.[16] Between Penrith and Keswick, in the vicinity of the known marching-camp at Troutbeck, lies a newly recognised fort site. Although not firmly dated, this fort had a rampart of clay blocks, and would fit the policing network. At some later date this fort was reduced in size.[17]

Relatively large-scale excavations were carried out at Ambleside (Waterhead) earlier in the century, and revealed a slightly irregular rectangular fort defended by clay ramparts. Outside there were two and, in places, three ditches. The central range of buildings was uncovered, though relating to a later stone-built phase of the fort. On the basis of the pottery the foundation of the fort has been assigned to the late Flavian period.[18] It is, however, worth noting that during site-clearance in 1982 approximately half a mile to

the north of the fort, features were observed which would not be inconsistent with a defensive system, though associated pottery was largely second century in date.

The position of the Ambleside fort at the head of Lake Windermere emphasises its peculiar advantage in that men and materials could be carried to the fort by ship independently of the road system. This in its turn serves to emphasise the continuing elusiveness of Roman sites in southern Cumbria which would have been linked to Ambleside by the lake. It is worth noting that in the 1970s, divers at the north end of Lake Windermere recognised large worked and perforated stones which would not be inconsistent with jetty-structures.

Presumably as part of the policing arrangements for the Lake District, a road was eventually driven through from Ambleside to the coast at Ravenglass. Although we now

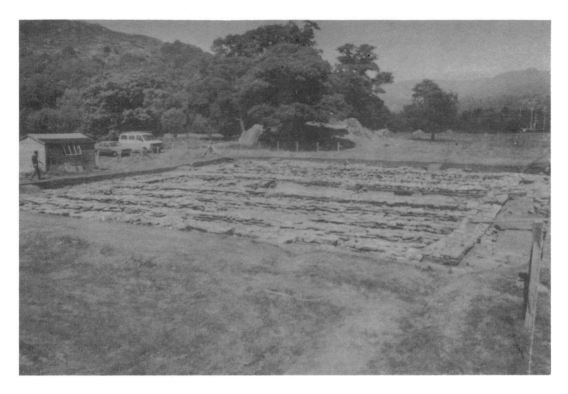

Plate 24. Ambleside: the fort granaries.

know that the latter site is of Hadrianic date, the intermediate fort at Hardknott is now regarded as having a Trajanic foundation.[19] This almost square fort is superbly sited with excellent visibility down Eskdale to the sea. The fort is stone-built, although it is assumed that a rampart-bank was originally provided and it had two ditches where necessary: on parts of the site, however, natural features obviated the need to cut ditches. Excavation of interior features revealed two phases of barrack-block – timber and stone.

Ravenglass[20] will be discussed more fully in its coastal context in the next chapter, but for the present purpose it is sufficient to say that the most recent excavations suggest that a mid-Hadrianic fort was preceded by an early Hadrianic fortlet on a different alignment. The dating of the other coastal forts is hazardous: Maryport, of which a stone wall and rampart have been recovered, appears on

coin and pottery evidence to be a late Flavian or, more likely, Trajanic foundation.[21] Of Moresby, Burrow Walls and Beckfoot, little is known, apart from the Hadrianic building-inscription from Moresby,[22] which has prompted the plausible suggestion[23] that on the coastal system some at least of the forts may have represented a later addition – as, of course, they did on Hadrian's Wall itself.

Further south, recent work at Water-crook,[24] although largely confined to the *vicus*, has suggested that the first phase, recognised in a clay-and-turf rampart, should not be placed earlier than late Flavian times. On the east angle, the outer defences consisted of three ditches: between the first and second was a palisade and a stone bank. The fort, which is nearly square, was protected on three sides by a bow of the River Kent, prompting the suggestion that it, rather than Hardknott,

Plate 25. Hardknott: the fort.

may be MEDIBOGDO of the *Ravenna Cosmography* – the name meaning 'fort in the middle of a bow' which closely describes Watercrook's disposition.

Thus consolidation work in the Lake District had the effect of driving east–west policing lines from the main north–south route in the direction of the coast. Field work also suggests the linking of some of these sites by north–south roads, which would thus have the effect of imposing an informal 'grid' on the area. One unanswered question concerns the southern fringes of the Lakes: no sites have been recovered, although the volume of finds in the Cartmel and Barrow areas suggests the possible existence of sites in Furness. It is similarly possible that sites await discovery on the coastline of southern Cumbria – for example, between Moresby and Ravenglass, and between Ravenglass and Barrow. In the former case it is worth noting the substantial amount of material to have come from the Beckermet area.[25]

The picture across Stainmore[26] in the consolidation period is unclear. At Greta Bridge, occupation from late Flavian times is assumed on the basis of finds, whilst at Bowes the elaborate Flavian (Agricolan) rampart was modified, though at a date not certainly proved. The fort at Brough, as noted above, has produced no clear evidence of its structural sequence, though its long-term importance is attested by the large collection of lead sealings of various army units found there. Kirkby Thore certainly had a second phase turf-and-clay rampart, though its date is uncertain.

Further south, other Pennine routes received attention: the probable Agricolan fort at Long Preston, a six-acre structure defended by a turf rampart, was at an unspecified time replaced by a smaller (three-acre) fort, also defended by a turf rampart.[27] Castleshaw, too, was reduced in size – the Agricolan fort of three acres being replaced by one of 0.6 acres built inside the earlier fort: whilst the second fort was undoubtedly of the second century, the exact date of its construction is unclear.[28] The changes of size, noted here and elsewhere in the north-west, must surely indicate considerable garrison-modifications over the years.

Whilst consolidation in Cumbria basically meant the laying out of a new fort-system, the military framework of Lancashire and Cheshire already existed. At Burrow-in-Lonsdale it appears that the presumed Agricolan turf-and-timber fort was modified and realigned, but at what date cannot be determined.[29] It is not unreasonable, however, to assume that a fair life-span for a turf-and-timber fort might have been twenty to twenty-five years before major modification and repair were required. In this case, provided that there was not a break in occupation at Burrow, a Trajanic date for the modifications would seem reasonable.

At the mouth of the Lune, Lancaster too underwent modification; in this case, a Trajanic building inscription[30] gives a clear indication and is presumably to be associated with the clay rampart and stone wall resting on a bevelled plinth course observed to the north of the old Vicarage. As noted above, this line of defence represented an enlargement of the earliest fort, and possibly its re-orientation through 90 degrees so that the main gate moved from the east to the north. Similarly, traces of the eastern gateway of a stone fort were excavated close to the junction of Church Street and China Street.

The Ribble forts also underwent modification. The addition of a stone wall to the first-phase rampart at Kirkham could conceivably have been Trajanic.[31] At Ribchester the evident complication of the site makes interpretation far more difficult. It is clear that the fort went through a number of modifications whilst retaining turf-and-timber construction. These modifications may have included a re-alignment through 90 degrees, which may also have involved a change in size and garrison. Evidence does exist to show that the Asturian cavalry, apparently based at Ribchester in the late first and early second centuries, was moved to Hadrian's Wall. It was to this unit that the famous parade-helmet belonged.

Further, the coin-series from Ribchester is not inconsistent with a break in occupation at some time in the Hadrianic period. Later in the second century AD, part of the consignment of Danubian Sarmatians, sent to Britain by Marcus Aurelius, was deployed at Ribchester. This may indicate further structural modifications, which apparently included the addition to the original turf rampart of a stone fort-wall which has been recovered in some, but not all, of the excavations. The stone phase evidently therefore belongs to the re-aligned fort, and it is assumed that the stone granaries which are visible at the rear of the Museum were part of this later fort-phase. The stone-building may be as late as Severan – (that is, early third century) – in date.32 A further importance of Ribchester is deduced from the form of the name of the site which is given in the *Ravenna Cosmography* as BRESNETENACI VETERANORUM.

The name implies a settlement of especial significance outside the fort, the body of which was made up of discharged soldiers. There has been much speculation regarding the purpose and effect of these, including the possibility that land was allocated to them in the Fylde (see below in chapter 6). Although no explicit indication of their presence has emerged from the archaeological record, it is possible that bank-and-ditch features which have been observed in two locations at a distance from the fort could be part of the defences provided for a settlement which had a quasi-military purpose.

On the southern side of the Ribble estuary, the site at Walton-le-Dale appears to have changed its purpose in this period. As we have seen, there are indications that it started as a

Plate 26. Hardknott: the parade ground.

Plate 27. Lancaster: building-inscription of Trajan's reign (Lancaster City Museum and Art Gallery). The inscription reads: 'To the Emperor Nerva Trajan Caesar Augustus Germanicus Dacicus, Consul . . . saluted as *Imperator*'.

fort until the earliest years of the Flavian period. After a break of occupation which lasted until the end of the first century, a new phrase of activity is apparent in the form of long, rectangular, shed-like buildings, constructed of timber. The regularity of these is persuasive of a military origin and purpose, though no clear traces that revealed that purpose emerged during the excavation of the site. It is perhaps best to suggest that the buildings were for the storage presumably of military supplies prior to their deployment elsewhere in the north-west. The site retained this character into the early third century AD, after which signs of occupation at Walton-le-Dale are far more ephemeral.

At Manchester, recent excavations[33] have demonstrated two turf-and-timber phases, the later of the two representing an enlargement of the fort from approximately four to five acres, apparently early in the second century. The mid-second century – possibly *c.* AD 165 – saw the addition of a stone wall to the later rampart. The same structural sequence has been observed both in the western defences and in the area of the north gateway. Further south at Northwich,[34] two phases of fort were recognised – an Agricolan phase which lasted until early in the second century, which was followed by the building of a wall to the front of the rampart. The commencement-date of phase II was not

precisely placed, but is probably Antonine. The site's later industrial activity will be discussed below (in chapter 6).

Excavations of the legionary fortress at Chester[35] have shown that it, too, shared in the work of consolidation: as noted above, the original fortification of Chester clearly goes back to Neronian times, but the Abbey Green excavations showed that the Flavian fortress itself underwent a number of modifications before the Trajanic rebuilding in stone, which is recorded on an inscription.[36]

Thus it can be seen that in Lancashire and Cheshire the consolidation-period represented a chronologically fairly uniform process of rebuilding and often enlarging Agricola's forts early in the Trajanic period; this fact incidentally can be regarded as confirmation of Tacitus' observation about Agricola's good eye for fort placement.[37]

It is stated by Tacitus that the results of Agricola's campaigns in their effects on the native population were dramatic – in terms of the abandonment of hostility and the acceptance of garrisons. This certainly implies a rapid establishment of peace: in a sense, the growth outside the forts of civilian settlements (*vici*), which were presumably in the main undefended, tends to confirm this. It can be shown that the majority of the forts saw *vici* established very soon after their own initial foundation. We also find that the manufacture and provision of building- and other material for the army, which was initially established perhaps on an *ad hoc* basis were, during the consolidation period, centralised. Whilst the evidence of industrial sites will be discussed more fully later, it is certainly relevant to the present purpose that individual manufacturing sites such as Holt (for Chester), Quernmore (for Lancaster), Muncaster (for Hardknott / Ravenglass), Brampton (for Old Church, Brampton), and Scalesceugh[38] were perhaps at least partly superseded by the growth of much larger manufacturing- and supply-centres – for example, Wilderspool, which appears to have started in the late Flavian / Trajanic period.[39] As will be shown later, there is reason to suppose that Wilderspool at any rate relied on native workers: the same may perhaps be said of 'industrial areas' within the *vici*: work at Manchester, Northwich and Middlewich has produced evidence of industrial activity in close connection with military sites. Whilst it may be the case at Northwich and Middlewich that this work followed military evacuation, at Manchester the 'industrial estate' was clearly part of the *vicus* and contemporary with the fort.[40] At the latter site, the movement of suitable raw materials to the site itself certainly implies settled conditions, possibly over a considerable area.[41]

However, whilst the work of Agricola and his successors certainly represents overall a positive achievement, and whilst, as we have seen, there is evidence which implies settled conditions, it is nonetheless true that the military could not afford to relax: a tight 'policing' network had been constructed, although this could of course break down, particularly in areas where movement was difficult. As we have seen, the evidence of field-work and excavation, combined with the comment of Spartianus, shows that conditions in the north of the region in the early second century had become tense and dangerous – perhaps because of further troop withdrawals in connection with Trajan's Dacian and Parthian wars. It is certainly evident that Hadrian's reappraisal in AD 117 showed him that the Trajanic level of military momentum was neither desirable nor practicable. Further, there is some evidence from early imperial coin-hoards in Lancashire[42] that conditions had become less settled in the south of the region also.

It is clear that Hadrian 'stopped the rot' – initially by intervention through his governor, Pompeius Falco. The longer-term and more radical solution, which may in fact be regarded as the culmination of consolidation, was the building of a new frontier – this time not a road, but a continuous barrier – Hadrian's Wall.

Footnotes – Chapter 4

1. *Histories* I. 2.
2. For recent discussions of the possible site of this battle, see Hanson 1987, 127ff and Maxwell, 1990.
3. *Scriptores Historiae Augustae* (SHA), *Life of Hadrian* 5,2; the 'Writers of the Augustan History' produced biographies of emperors of the second and third centuries; the quality of these is extremely variable, although Spartianus, who composed the *Life of Hadrian*, is considered to be one of the better authors.
4. Suetonius, *Life of Domitian* 10.
5. *Satires* IV.127.

6. *Satires* XIV.196.
7. Hill, 1970, 53.
8. Hanson, 1987, 53.
9. Breeze and Dobson, 1976, 20ff.
10. Birley E. B., 1951.
11. *Britannia* XVI (1985), 276.
12. Birley E. B., 1963; Charlesworth, 1965.
13. Bellhouse, 1960a; Jones M. J., 1975, 135.
14. Austen, 1991.
15. *JRS* LVII (1967), 177; *JRS* LVIII (1968), 179.
16. Jones M. J., 1975, 164.
17. Jones M. J., 1975, 180.
18. Hartley, 1966, 12; for recent work on the fort, see *Britannia* XXI (1990), 320; the work to the north of the fort is summarised in *Britannia* XIV (1983), 292.
19. Hartley, 1966, 12; *JRS* LV (1965), 203; Jones M. J., 1975, 154f.
20. Potter, 1979, 48f.
21. Jarrett, 1976.
22. *RIB* 801; this inscription is dated to post-AD 128.
23. Potter, 1979, 359.
24. For the excavations of 1974–5 and a discussion of results see Potter, 1979.
25. Shotter, 1980, 163.
26. Greta Bridge (Jones M. J., 1975, 154); Bowes (Jones, M. J., 1975, 130f); Brough-under-Stainmore (Richmond, 1936; Jones M. J., 1977); Kirkby Thore (Jones M. J., 1975, 158; Gibbons, 1989).
27. Jones M. J., 1975, 162f.
28. Jones M. J., 1975, 140; *Britannia* XIX (1988), 444; XX (1989), 280.
29. Jones M. J., 1975, 134.
30. *RIB* 604; Shotter and White, 1990.
31. Jones M. J., 1975, 159.
32. For a summary of the most recent work at Ribchester, see *Britannia* XXI (1990), 328. Earlier work has been published in Edwards and Webster, 1985–8.
33. *Britannia* XI (1980), 364; XIII (1982), 353; XVII (1986), 385.
34. *Britannia* XV (1984), 288.
35. Thompson, 1965, 24ff.
36. *RIB* 464; *Britannia* IX (1978), 429f.
37. *Life of Agricola* 22.
38. Holt (Grimes, 1930); Quernmore (Jones and Shotter, 1988, 85ff.); Muncaster (Bellhouse, 1960b); Brampton (Hogg, 1965); Scalesceugh (*Britannia* II (1971), 251).
39. Thompson, 1965, 67–87; Hinchcliffe and Williams, 1992.
40. Jones G. D. B., 1974.
41. Jones G. D. B., 1974, 153f.
42. Shotter, 1978b; Shotter, 1990, 129ff.

5. The Northern Frontier

The events in the northern frontier area in the first two decades of the second century are, as we have seen, riddled with interpretative problems. The only certain element is that there was disturbance – possibly throughout the whole of the north-west. It seems that this trouble had first to be dealt with, and then a more lasting answer found to it. By inference we can assume that Hadrian's view was that, alone, the Stanegate system was inadequate.

Hadrian himself came to Britain in AD 121 or 122 – evidently almost the first of his long series of imperial visits.[1] Apart from the introduction of a new policy, two further, presumably related, changes may be discerned: the governor Quintus Pompeius Falco was replaced by Aulus Platorius Nepos (AD 122–5), and Legion IX *Hispana* at York was replaced by Legion VI *Victrix*, previously garrisoned at Vetera (Xanten) on the Rhine. Nepos' earlier career had given him service as governor of Lower Germany, whilst the legion must have had extensive experience of frontier works on the Rhine (*Limes Germanicus*), and it has been suggested[2] that the legion came straight from the Rhine to the Tyne. Although Legion IX *Hispana* had not over the years had a happy time in Britain and may well have suffered in the recent disturbances, the story of its disappearance is romantic fiction. That the new policy was Hadrian's own is attested by his biographer, Spartianus: 'He made for Britain, where he set right many things and – the first to do so – drew a wall along a length of eighty miles to separate barbarians and Romans'.

A detailed discussion of Hadrian's Wall is beyond the scope of the present work; comment will thus be restricted to more general observations. It is evident that in the first instance Hadrian's Wall was seen as a unity with the Stanegate, since although small patrols (perhaps approximately twenty men each) were housed in the milecastles, the main bodies of troops at first remained in the Stanegate forts. Whilst the Stanegate ran through the valleys of the Tyne, Irthing and Eden rivers, the wall occupied the northern crests of those valleys. In all, then, this will have had the effect of retaining the policing potential of the traditional *limes* and added to it the ability both to see and deal with threats from the north. It was thus in effect a 'barrier-*limes*' that cut through northern Brigantian territory, controlling traffic and the interconnection of groups whose combination we must assume to have been considered hazardous. The wall, with the enormous strategic advantage it gained from such natural features as the Great Whin Sill, will have greatly enhanced the policing potential of the Stanegate since it will have relieved pressure from the northern flank of that line.

The original plan seems to have included the wall itself, a ditch to the north (not cut where natural features made it unnecessary), and milecastles every Roman mile, between each pair of which were two square turrets. With installations so closely spaced, lateral communications along the wall were clearly at a premium. The wall eventually ran from Wallsend in the east to Bowness-on-Solway in the west; its eastern two-thirds (as far as the Irthing Gap) were built of stone, whilst the western third was of turf, with installations of turf-and-timber construction. A fragmentary wooden inscription from Milecastle 50 places this work in Nepos' governorship.

The reason for the change in building-materials on the western sector has often been discussed – with various solutions proposed. Possibly it was the paucity of good building-stone or limestone for mortar, at least, close enough at hand to make quarrying a worthwhile and / or safe undertaking. This might be of relevance if, as many have supposed, the chief problems with local tribesmen lay in the west. We should, however, remember that for most of the occupation of the north to that time, turf and timber had been regarded as perfectly adequate materials: we should not therefore necessarily assume that in the Roman mind the materials of the western sector were markedly inferior in capability to the stone of the east. The chief problem would be a longer-term one – namely, that the turf-and-timber structures would presumably require major renovation before the stonework.

Platorius Nepos was replaced as governor in AD 125 or 126; at about this time the decision was evidently made to bring the main bodies of troops on to the wall itself and to build forts for them there. Recent excavation at Bowness-on-Solway[3] has suggested that the process may not have been chronologically uniform over the entire wall, and certainly Carrawburgh, by its relationship with the *vallum*, can be shown to have been an 'after-thought' (*c.* AD 133). In effect, therefore, the Stanegate forts of Chesterholm (Vindolanda), Nether Denton and Brampton were advanced to Housesteads, Great Chesters, Birdoswald and Castlesteads, whilst at Carvoran the wall and the Stanegate were close enough for the fort to be retained. At Carlisle, a new fort was built at Stanwix, although recent excavation suggests that this did not mean the loss of a garrison at Carlisle itself. On the western Stanegate, Burgh I,

Plate 28. Hadrian's Wall: Housesteads fort.

Figure 4. Sites occupied at the death of Hadrian.

Finglandrigg, and Kirkbride were advanced respectively to Burgh II, Drumburgh and Bowness-on-Solway. The relationship between the 'fort phase' and the 'pre-fort phase' has been convincingly demonstrated by the discovery that some of the forts overlie already existing wall-installations – for example, at Housesteads.[4] We should also note that in the western sector the turf wall was equipped with turf-and-timber forts; recent excavations have demonstrated that, contrary to previous expectations, a turf-and-timber phase preceded the stone fort at Birdoswald.[5]

To the south of the forts, and evidently part of the same plan, ran the *vallum*, the name used for the feature since Bede's time. This consisted of a flat-bottomed ditch, some 8 feet deep, with steep sides. When kept clean, it would have been extremely hard for an intruder to extricate himself from it: north and south of the *vallum*-ditch were cleared areas (or berms), bounded by continuous mounds of earth made up of the upcast from the ditch and carefully revetted with turf. The feature, which runs the whole length of the wall on its southern side (except for the eastern extension to Wallsend) was 20 feet wide overall. Its purpose has been much discussed, but it would appear to have demarcated a military zone on the southern side of the wall, and possibly acted as a 'man-trap' – thus either keeping out unauthorised people or getting them into a position where they would not easily be able to get across to the north of the wall, and perhaps trap them until they were rounded up by patrols. An alternative explanation of its purpose is that the *vallum*-ditch provided a concealed communications-route, perhaps for covert deployment of troops.

The *vallum* may perhaps give us a clue as to

Plate 29. Hadrian's Wall: Birdoswald fort.

45

why the 'fort-phase' of the wall was undertaken: a military zone which consisted of the wall, the Stanegate and intervening territory was perhaps too wide in most areas for convenience or efficiency as well as security. For example, the distance between Kirkbride and its 'wall-equivalent', Bowness-on-Solway, is four miles. In this connection, it is worth noting that even in a communications role the Stanegate was superseded by the military way which ran in the wall / *vallum* corridor.

The whole system was in place probably by the mid-130s. However, the replacement of turf-and-timber by stone structures is hard to place chronologically. It has been suggested that this work may have been done late in Hadrian's reign,[6] or possibly after the evacuation of the Antonine Wall in the 160s. In recent years, however, excavation at Bowness-on-Solway failed to provide a firm date for the inception of the stone-phase, whilst those at Birdoswald have suggested that at that fort the work could be as late as the Severan period.[7] It might therefore be safest to assume that this particular type of modification did not belong to a single plan, but was carried out over a period. Indeed, the record of building-inscriptions from Hadrian's Wall suggests that there was a near-continuous building-programme from the 160s into the early years of the third century.[8]

Three outpost forts were provided in the west to the north of the Wall – at Birrens, Netherby and Bewcastle. It is argued[9] that these were not 'early-warning' forts, but placed to protect that part of Brigantian territory which was cut off by the Wall – an argument which receives some force from the discovery of the Romanised *Brigantia*-relief at Birrens. It is further argued that since these forts are tied to Hadrian's Wall by a road, which runs to Milecastle 50 rather than to Birdoswald, they were part of the original *plan*, though not necessarily actually built until the mid-Hadrianic period. Notable amongst these is Bewcastle, which abandons the normal rectangular shape in favour of an irregular polygon encompassing a hill-top: this was presumably intended to give it good visibility in what might be expected to be troubled terrain.[10]

The wall-forts were all of a size to accommodate complete units.[11] The average acreage is approximately five, with the two largest at Bowness-on-Solway and Stanwix (9.32). Despite some confusions over the names of Hadrian's Wall forts,[12] there seems no doubt that Stanwix housed the milliary *Ala Petriana*, and was the Wall's command centre – a point which receives added weight from its close proximity to Carlisle, where recent excavation has shown a continued military presence in the second century, and has revealed evidence for the presence there of detachments at least of all three British legions.

Also, as we have seen, a writing-tablet from Vindolanda alludes to the presence at Carlisle of a high-ranking officer, known as a *centurio regionarius*. It has been calculated that the Wall-installations will in all have required around 11,500 men: this will obviously have required some movement of garrisons from existing bases.

Hadrian's successor, Antoninus Pius, once again initiated a forward policy: his views may reflect a gradually less secure situation in southern Scotland, or the desire to make southern Scotland more of a barrier against the real enemy in the north. Further, as a relatively unknown senator, he, like Claudius, may have felt the need to bolster his military reputation. A detailed study of the Antonine Wall[13] would clearly be out of place in the present volume: it will thus be treated only in so far as it affected the situation in northern England.

The removal of the armies northwards came in AD 143 under the governor, Quintus Lollius Urbicus, and possibly in response to some pressure on the northern frontier.[14] It is clear enough that this entailed the substantial decommissioning of Hadrian's Wall, for

Hartley's study of the samian ware from both walls shows that they were not held contemporaneously; it has been shown, for example, that the *vallum*-ditch was filled with turf to make it easy to cross. At the same time it has long been recognised that some, at least, of the Antonine Wall forts enjoyed two periods of occupation.[15] It now seems clear – and the numismatic evidence can be shown to support this[16] – that the two periods have to be seen within a shorter time-span than has traditionally been thought.

It is evident that the first period ended, probably violently, *c.* AD 155: it is likely that Antoninus' 'dejected' BRITANNIA coin of AD 154–5 reflects this. It is now reasonable to assume that the second period was brief, and possibly a 'punitive' measure launched by Marcus Aurelius on his accession and terminated as soon as it had achieved its objectives – perhaps *c.* AD 163. The circumstances of this are not clear, though disturbance in the north must be assumed, and indeed, as will be seen, evidently continued intermittently throughout the rest of the second century. However, the notion of a major Brigantian revolt during Antoninus' reign has recently been convincingly challenged.[17]

The existence of Roman installations on the coast of Cumbria has long been known; however, the questions of their extent, complexity and evolution have been the subject of a great deal of research and debate in recent years.[18] A concentrated period since the mid-1950s of aerial reconnaissance, ground-work and mainly relatively small-scale excavations has revealed the existence on the coastline westward from Bowness-on-Solway of occasional auxiliary forts, fortlets every Roman mile, and two towers between each pair of milefortlets: besides these, there is evidence of linear features in the form of a road with flanking ditches and palisades. Some excavation has taken place at many of the surviving sites, but few have been extensively sampled; these are, Milefortlets 1 (Biglands), 5 (Cardurnock) and 21 (Swarthy Hill) and Tower 4B (Cardurnock).[19]

The excavations (excluding those at the forts) have generally pointed to three main phases of occupation; further, the excavation on the site of Tower 4B has revealed a development-sequence for the coastal defence arrangements which also appears to fall into three phases separated by intervals of disuse. At that site the *first* phase was represented by a palisade or fence, fronted (on the seaward side) by a ditch, and having along it, regularly spaced between each pair of milefortlets, small 'platforms' constructed of turf and clay. The *second* phase consisted of a new palisade, built slightly inland of the first, which cut through the 'platform' of the first phase. This, too, was associated with a road, and was fronted by a re-cut ditch. The *third* phase had no running barrier, but was represented by a stone-built tower nearer to the sea and overlying the now in-filled ditch.

Features comparable to these have been located further south at Silloth;[20] here, there were two palisades, running north–south though not quite parallel to each other, and two ditches which flanked a north–south coastal road. The palisades consisted of a trench packed with clay into which at close intervals double posts had been pushed. It is assumed that these posts supported wattle sections, and that the whole can be seen to fit a description of Hadrianic frontiers to be found in Spartianus' biography[21] – 'During this period, and frequently at other times, in a great many places where the barbarians are separated off not by rivers but by frontier-barriers, he set them apart by great stakes driven deep into the ground, and fastened together in the manner of a palisade'. This description, which has usually been taken to apply to arrangements in Germany, but which clearly, from the above text, is not meant to be limited to one area alone, can be seen to have obvious relevance to the palisades located on the coast of Cumbria.

How far along the coast similar arrangements exist is hard to say, but it is clear that

Plate 30. Birdoswald: the west gate, with its esceptionally fine masonry.

Plate 31. Birdoswald: the south granary.

different areas show evidence of different treatment: for example, running towards Milefortlet 1 (Biglands) from the east, are two ditches which diverge to join the north and south ditches of the milefortlet. It is assumed that these ditches, therefore, provided a corridor in which the coastal installations were located.[22] Further research, however, has suggested that from Milefortlet 3 (Pasture House), or possibly Milefortlet 2 (North Plain), only a single forward ditch was cut.[23] It is also clear that since Milefortlet 1 (Biglands) is in excess of a Roman mile to the west of Bowness-on-Solway, the two systems (that is, Hadrian's Wall and the coastal system) were not planned in complete conjunction.

The excavation of Milefortlet 1 (Biglands)

has demonstrated a sequence of three periods[24] – a sequence which has been shown to be compatible with other milefortlet sites where excavation has taken place. Owing to the sparse nature of the dating evidence, these three periods have to be asserted rather tentatively, apart from the fact that all fall within the second century AD. It is reasonably certain that phase I should be placed in the period c. AD 125–40, thus corresponding approximately with the building and first Antonine abandonment of Hadrian's Wall. Given the new, but now generally accepted, sequence on the Antonine Wall,[25] there is no objection to phase II of Biglands being placed between Antonine Wall I and II, with phase III of Biglands commencing c. AD 163 and extending until c. AD 180 (or possibly c. AD 200). At a number of the coastal installations, three phases have been detected, and at none is the dating evidence inconsistent with the chronological model based upon the excavations at Biglands. Further, it is probably not unreasonable to relate the three phases of the milefortlet to the phases recovered at the site of Tower 4B (Cardurnock).

The character of the milefortlets so far examined varies: it would appear that with the certain exception of Milefortlet 5 (Cardurnock: 1,130 square metres) and possibly also of Milefortlet 9 (Skinburness)[26] which are larger than average, the milefortlets' areas are approximately 300–350 square metres in each case – that is, capable of holding a small patrol group. The larger ones are presumably to be explained on the basis of their special positions which required larger than normal garrisons – perhaps a *centuria*. Although it cannot be said that all of the sites conform to a similar structural pattern, it would appear that most have ramparts of turf and clay, defended by a palisade running on the inner side of a single ditch. At Swarthy Hill (Milefortlet 21), however, excavation has revealed a rampart of less substantial construction, consisting of an inner and outer face of turf containing an infill of earth. They

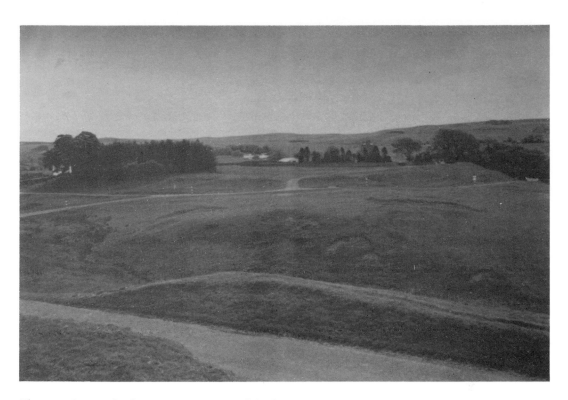

Plate 32. Bewcastle: the western ramparts of the fort.

are entered front and rear by six-post timber gateways. The interior buildings are mostly rather unimpressive in appearance, resembling 'sheds' of turf and timber, with cooking facilities. These were presumably the barrack-buildings of the fortlets.

Phases I and II bore a close resemblance to each other, although distinguished by a period of deliberate demolition. Phase III, however, was considerably smaller; the inland gateway appears to have been closed, and the rampart pierced by a single entrance giving on to the coast; this entrance was structurally markedly less impressive than the earlier gateways. Similar deterioration and size-reductions have been observed elsewhere than at Biglands.

The coastal auxiliary forts have similarly produced little firm evidence for the construction-dates and subsequent chronologies. Neither Beckfoot nor Burrow Walls offer any basis for speculation; Moresby,

however, has at least produced a building-inscription dating to the last decade of Hadrian's reign (AD 128–38).[27] A Hadrianic foundation-date has, as a result of the excavations of 1966,[28] been assigned to Maryport, although it is worth pointing out that the evidence of coin-loss at least would support an earlier – perhaps late Flavian – date. Further south, the evidence for Ravenglass is strongly suggestive of a Hadrianic foundation-date – possibly even late in that reign. This evidence might suggest that the whole of the coastal installations were constructed later than Hadrian's Wall, or possibly that, as on Hadrian's Wall itself, the auxiliary forts represent a revision of an earlier plan;[29] neither hypothesis of course precludes the possibility that one fort at least – (that is, Maryport) – pre-dated all the other installations along the coast.

A further problem concerns the overall extent of the coastal installations: the

Plate 33. The Cumbrian coast north of Maryport.

support in the evidence for this. Indeed, it may be more likely that the defences were conceived in two parts – north and south of *Moricambe*.

The traditional view has been that the southerly extent of the coastal fortifications was to St Bees Head – a view which was thought to have achieved apparent support from the discovery of a possible milefortlet at Harrington Parks,[30] which has a sight of St Bees; the nature of the Harrington site, however, has yet to be determined. Further, the existence of a fortlet, comparable in size to Biglands, beneath the Hadrianic fort at Ravenglass[31] has prompted the suggestion that the system may continue considerably further south than is sometimes supposed. However, a rather stronger argument relies on the changing nature of the coastline south of Maryport, and favours the tower at Rise How as the southern *terminus*. A compromise may

generally accepted enumeration of sites presupposes the existence of a continuous, coherent, 'system' of defences from Bowness-on-Solway, and assumes that they skirted round the bay of *Moricambe* although there is no

Plate 34. Maryport: the fort.

Plate 35. The Biglands milefortlet (photograph, T. W. Potter).

be suggested: it has been shown that the hinterland which is bounded on its southern side by the road from Carlisle to Maryport supported substantial rural settlement. We have seen that in the first half-century of occupation (c. AD 70–120), care had been taken to protect this area on both its coastal and inland flanks from those who might seek to pillage or destroy. Clearly, this risk grew less severe as the coastline itself began to provide a greater natural defence. Where the cliffs were substantial, an occasional watch-tower may have sufficed. We might therefore expect to find further isolated sections of defensive structures where the nature of the coastline merited it, and where the hinterland supported substantial settlement. The lower reaches of the Esk to its estuary at Ravenglass might be regarded as such an area. Further areas could be postulated, and in considering both this and the possibility of sites lost to

coastal change, we have to remember that high-tide level on the west coast was considerably higher in the Roman period than it is now.[32]

In short, therefore, we are beginning to see progress on all three of the initial questions posed concerning the coastal system – its extent, complexity and evolution. The first of these requires more work, whilst the other two, although presenting a clear enough picture for the second century, are further complicated by a limited amount of fourth-century evidence – which we shall consider below (in chapter 7).

The provision of the Stanegate fortifications, then Hadrian's Wall and the coastal system, and then the Antonine Wall, must clearly have necessitated great flexibility in troop-disposition in the north. In this matter our lack of detailed chronologies for so many sites severely hampers discussion. It is clear that some of the construction and perhaps garrison-duties could be, and were, undertaken by the legions. It is similarly clear that in broad terms the Stanegate forts lost their garrisons when Hadrian's Wall was built, although this cannot be taken as a firm rule, since the *Notitia Dignitatum* in its 'wall sub-section' includes Vindolanda,[33] properly a Stanegate fort. Further, we have seen that Hadrian's Wall and the coastal system were not held contemporaneously with the Antonine Wall.[34] These factors will certainly have helped to lend the flexibility necessary for providing garrisons for these frontier arrangements.

It is also known that at some stage in the second half of the second century, following Marcus Aurelius' Danube wars, Sarmatian troops were sent to reinforce the garrisons in Britain.[35] At least some of these were in

Plate 36. Silloth: the palisade (photograph, G. D. B. Jones.

garrison at Ribchester. Further, from Hadrian's time onwards, it was a growing practice to supplement the regular legions and auxiliary *cohortes* and *alae* with irregular units from border areas which are generally known as *numeri* and *cunei*. Of course, for sites where a sufficient body of evidence has been recovered we can sometimes see characteristic fluctuations in the ceramic and numismatic evidence to indicate temporary abandonments or reductions. It is reasonably clear, for example, that Ribchester lost its garrison when Hadrian's Wall was built, as did Lancaster, to facilitate Antoninus' advance into Scotland.[36] Some Pennine forts (such as Castleshaw and Brough-on-Noe) may have lost their garrisons, whilst other forts - for example, Watercrook – have provided evidence of relatively complex garrison-patterns, with periods of activity interspersed with periods of apparent demilitarisation.

It has been postulated that a number of sites may have seen reductions or losses of garrisons in the Trajanic / Hadrianic period: for example, Ambleside, Watercrook, Lancaster, Maryport, Kirkby Thore.[37] Further, the evidence of building-sequences and of samian pottery from Watercrook strongly indicates that the fort was being built in stone when the Antonine advance into Scotland began, was then abandoned, and reoccupied following the final withdrawal from Scotland *c.* AD 163. Epigraphic evidence further suggests (in the form of building inscriptions of the governorship of Calpurnius Agricola, AD 163–6) that Ribchester and Hardknott[38] were being rebuilt at this stage, from which we might reasonably infer garrison-loss or reduction in connection with the second-century frontier movements.

In these few sites for which we have some evidence, we probably see the 'tip of the iceberg' of the Roman army's flexibility. Units could easily be moved: and it is quite likely, in view of the number of very small sites on Hadrian's Wall and the coastal system, *and*, as is now emerging,[39] on the

Plate 37. Ribchester: second-century coin-hoard, found in the excavation of 1978.

Antonine Wall too, that much of the detailed garrisoning must have been accomplished by taking small detachments from units whose main bases and headquarters' staffs remained elsewhere.

From the literary point of view, events of the later second century are ill-documented, and coin-loss figures, too (for monetary reasons), become less reliable indicators of occupation patterns. There is some evidence of disturbances amongst the Brigantes, although on what scale is unclear. It would, however, seem excessive to talk of a 'Brigantian rebellion'. That Commodus' governor, Ulpius Marcellus (AD 180–5), had to resist attacks from the north, is made clear by Dio Cassius, and by Commodus' issue of coins commemorating victory in Britain.[40] Also during Commodus' reign an inscription from Carlisle[41] records the slaughter of 'a band of barbarians' by the *Ala Augusta Petriana*: further, an undated tombstone from Ambleside[42] records the death of one Flavius Romanus, who was killed by the enemy inside his fort.

The death of Commodus in AD 192 ushered in a period of civil war and confusion during which the governor, Clodius Albinus (AD 191–6), used elements of the British garrison to further his own ambitions: the result was predictable for we find his successor, Virius Lupus (AD 197–201), having to buy off the northern tribes and being heavily involved in rebuilding in the Pennines[43] – whether following destruction or abandonment is hard to say, though the archaeological evidence from Ravenglass[44] certainly supports enemy attack at this time followed by immediate rebuilding. Continuing building-work on the frontier and in the hinterland under the Severan governors, Pudens and Senecio (AD 202–8), suggests continuing pressure from the north – which eventually brought the emperor himself to Britain to campaign in the north-east of Scotland. The events of the last quarter of the second century seem also to have led, as we have seen, to the decision to abandon most, if not all, of the smaller installations of the coastal system, presumably partly because they were no longer relevant and partly because their manpower may well have been required elsewhere.

Severus and his family based themselves at York for what was clearly intended to be the final solution to the long years of disturbance. It is clear that the chief trouble lay north of the Forth / Clyde isthmus, in the shape of the Maeatae, the third-century northern neighbours of Agricola's Caledonii. Severus' campaigns took little, if any, notice of southern Scotland, nor was the Antonine Wall reoccupied. In fact, it looks very like Agricola's final campaign repeated on the grand-scale – perhaps hoping to take the heart out of the Maeatae. Severus died at York in AD 211 before the work was complete, though his son and successor, Caracalla, did eventually produce a diplomatic solution which, though sneered at by ancient writers,[45] appears to have secured almost a century of peace in the north.

The garrison-pattern of north-west England during the third century is difficult to establish without much more excavation:[46] in any case, the ceramic and numismatic evidence provide far less clear indications than they do for earlier periods. We may well expect that the internal upheavals which preceded Severus' rise, coupled with his own great stress on the army as the source of his power, will have led to reorganisation of existing garrisons.

The establishment of peace will have given the opportunity for more flexible handling (that is, reduction and / or movement) of garrisons. Watercrook, for example, appears to have lost its garrison early in the third century, and to have remained unmanned until the late 260s or early 270s. At Lancaster, there is evidence of substantial rebuilding in the 260s,[47] presumably following a period of abandonment. Indeed, from the Severan period through to the 240s,[48] we find a large number of sites where rebuilding was taking place. As we have seen, although the garrison-pattern cannot be recovered in any detail, such evidence as there is for it, coupled with the rebuilding activity, strongly suggests large-scale redeployment. Evidently, too, there was now sufficient stability to allow for the withdrawal of garrisons from some parts of the north-west, including at least some of the forts of Hadrian's Wall.

However, as the third century wore on, as we have seen, some remanning took place. It may be assumed that the tensions experienced all over the Empire were beginning to find their expression in Britain also. However, these and other matters relating to the later years of occupation will be treated in a later chapter.

Footnotes – Chapter 5

1. *Scriptores Historiae Augustae, Life of Hadrian* 11, 2
2. Breeze and Dobson, 1976, 54.
3. Potter, 1979, 333f.
4. *JRS* XXXVI (1946), 134ff.
5. *Britannia* XXI (1990), 134ff.
6. Breeze and Dobson, 1976, 52f.
7. Potter, 1979, 321ff.
8. Potter, 1979, 362.
9. Breeze and Dobson, 1976, 43.
10. Austen, 1992.
11. Breeze and Dobson, 1976, 48.
12. Hassall, 1976; Shotter in Potter, 1979, 318.
13. Hanson and Maxwell, 1983.
14. *Scriptores Historiae Augustae, Life of Antoninus* 5.4.
15. Breeze, 1975
16. Shotter, 1976.
17. Hind, 1977; Hartley, 1980.
18. See particularly Higham and Jones, 1975; Bellhouse, 1981; Jones, 1982; Jones and Higham, 1985; Bellhouse, 1989.
19. Biglands (Potter, 1977); Cardurnock (Simpson and Hodgson, 1947); Tower 4B (Jones, 1982).
20. Jones, 1982, 293f.
21. *Scriptores Historiae Augustae, Life of Hadrian* 12.6.
22. Higham and Jones, 1975, 20ff.
23. Jones, 1982, 287.
24. Potter, 1977.
25. Breeze, 1975.

26. Bellhouse, 1954b, 36.
27. *RIB* 801.
28. Jarrett, 1976.
29. Potter, 1979, 359.
30. Jones, 1982, 296.
31. Potter, 1979, 14ff.
32. Jones, 1980; Jones, 1982, 291f.
33. The section on the western empire (40.32ff): the 'wall' section of the document is of disputed date (Gillam, 1949; Goodburn and Bartholomew, 1976).
34. Hartley, 1972.
35. Dio Cassius LXXII. 16 (narrated amongst the events of AD 176).
36. Shotter, 1979.
37. See Potter, 1979, 177 for individual references.
38. *RIB* 589 (Ribchester); *RIB* 793 (Hardknott).
39. Keppie and Walker, 1981.
40. Dio Cassius LXXIII, 8; for the coins, see *RIC* III (Commodus) 440 of AD 183–4.
41. *RIB* 946.
42. *JRS* LIII (1963), 160.
43. Hartley, 1980.
44. Dio Cassius LXXVI.5; Potter, 1979, 363.
45. Herodian III.15.6.
46. See Appendix II.
47. *RIB* 605; see Jones and Shotter, 1988, 208ff.
48. See Appendix III.

6. Soldiers and Civilians in the North-West

It was at one time assumed that in the wake of the military conquest of Britain there followed immigration by farmers from Europe anxious to capitalise on the 'rich pickings' to be had in the new province. Such a view was generated partly by the sophisticated organisation which the villa-system of lowland Britain seemed to imply, and partly by the evident luxury of life-style demonstrated by some of the villas. It is now appreciated that the villa-system was a natural development out of the pre-Roman organisation, that many villas were and remained extremely straightforward in style, and that the luxurious villas in general represent a level of wealth achieved by relatively few and only after a considerable period. Further, the observation of the Greek geographer, Strabo (writing in the early first century AD), that Iron-Age Britain produced an exportable surplus of grain[1] shows that whilst the architecture of the Iron-Age farm may not have been particularly impressive the methods employed by the farmers clearly were. It is not unreasonable to see these successful Iron-Age farmers as the ruling cliques of their tribes who represented socially and economically the class upon whom a system of local government in the new province could be based.

Such a picture is now widely accepted for lowland Britain; farming and other trades were stimulated by the presence of Roman troops who formed a 'market' which required satisfaction, as well as providing physical focal points on which economic and social intercourse were centred. An economic network was thus established which provided the basis for the physical and political organisation of the lowlands once the army moved on.

The Cotswolds offer in microcosm an excellent demonstration: in the early days of conquest, the area was policed through a legionary fortress at Gloucester and an auxiliary fort at Cirencester; together these guarded against any nationalistic activity which might have been based on hill-fort sites, such as Bagendon. Before long, military imperatives were less concerned with this area, and Romanisation began. By the end of the first century AD, the fortress and settlement at Gloucester was made into a *colonia*, a town high in the Roman urban hierarchy, but by definition largely self-sufficient. The real impact on the social, political and economic landscape was made by Cirencester: after the army moved on (in the early 70s), the civilian settlement which had established itself outside the fort was strong enough as a town to stand on its own feet. It had replaced Bagendon as the focus of local attention, and had developed to the point of being the natural administrative and economic centre of this part of Britain. Those who prospered and who on the basis of their prosperity could be entrusted with the tasks of local government were the descendants of those who in the 40s had used Bagendon and other such sites as the centres of their resistance to the new military occupation.

This in brief is a picture of Romanisation in lowland Britain during the first century AD: we need now to compare it with what we know of the north. Even though the close interdependence of Roman and native in lowland Britain has eventually been recognised, opinion has generally been slow to recognize that parts at least of the highland zone can be viewed in a similar way. Attention has been focussed on to the predominant military presence, and the native population has been dismissed with such words as 'sparse', 'backward', or 'recalcitrant'. As a result of more excavation of military and non-military sites, of substantial programmes of aerial reconnaissance, and of fresh evidence such as is provided by the Vindolanda writing-tablets, we are now in a much better position to assess the social and economic importance of the military presence in the north, and the relationship that developed between Roman and native in the highland zone; we can begin to see too what level of wealth was achieved by native farmers and, on the analogy of what happened further south, what kinds of responsibilities were entrusted to the rich and influential amongst the local population.

As a crucial part of this discussion we need to assess the changing military imperatives in the area. The 'Roman army' is a term which generates misconceptions both in fact and implication: it conjures up the notion of a ruthless foreign force, bent on the reduction to quiescence and serfdom of the native population amongst whom it worked. However, Rome could not afford to think of her army in that way, for she had not the resources to contemplate an army of the size that would be necessary if all provinces were treated in such a way as to make them seething hotbeds of discontent. In fact, genuine provincial rebellions against Rome were relatively rare occurrences, indicating that above all things once peace and stability were attained, there was much scope for flexibility of approaches. Tacitus might give the Caledonian chieftain, Calgacus, the dismissive words, 'they create a desolation and call it peace',[2] but it is evident that such would have been decidedly a minority view amongst Rome's subjects. The army was less an instrument of foreign tyranny than a police force whose activities were as much in the interests of local populations as of anyone else.

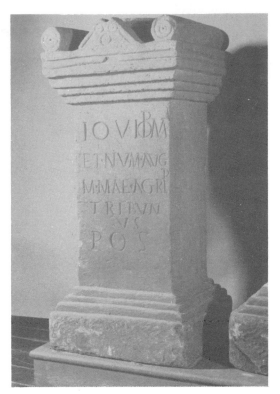

Plate 38. Maryport: altar dedicated to Jupiter Optimus Maximus (copyright, Senhouse Museum Trust). The inscription reads: 'To Jupiter, Best and Greatest, and to the Divine Spirit of the Emperor, Marcus Maenius Agrippa, the Tribune, set this up'.

For economic and political reasons, the Roman army was not allowed to grow endlessly; in fact, over the first two centuries AD, the average number of troops under arms was approximately 350,000 over the empire as a whole.[3] Of these perhaps ten per cent were committed to Britain – legions and auxiliary troops in approximately equal numbers. Three legions were posted permanently to Britain – VI *Victrix* at York (which in the early 120s replaced IX *Hispana*), II *Augusta* at Caerleon, and XX *Valeria Victrix* at Chester - though these could be used more flexibly with detachments ('vexillations') serving away from their main bases, as clearly happened in

Plate 39. Lancaster: inscription referring to a third-century rebuilding of the bath-house (Lancaster City Museum and Art Gallery). The inscription reads: 'For the Emperor [Postumus], on account of the rebuilding of the Bath-house and the restoring from ground-level of the Basilica which had collapsed through old age, for the Soldiers of the Sebosian Cavalry Regiment [Postumus's own], under Octavius Sabinus, Senator and Governor, and under Flavius Ammausius, Prefect of Cavalry: dedicated on 22 August, in the year in which Censor and Lepidus were Consuls, each for the second time'.

the building of the Hadrianic and Antonine Walls in the second century AD. The legions consisted of 5,500 men each, and were largely made up of infantry; all legionaries were Roman citizens, though this did not of course mean that they were by origin Roman, or even Italian. The deliberate spreading of Roman citizenship through the provinces of the empire meant that large numbers of men from all over the empire were eligible for service in the legions. Thus, in terms of the men who made them up, the legions were diverse units which brought great variety of custom and background to the provinces in which they served. It is likely that in time at least some Britons found their way into the legions, possibly serving in Britain itself.

Serving alongside the legions were units of auxiliary troops; these were organised into smaller groups than the legions – basically 500 or 1000 strong – and could be made up of cavalry (*alae*), infantry cohorts with some cavalry (*cohortes equitatae*), or cohorts which were solely infantry (*cohortes peditatae*). These too could be sub-divided, as clearly happened on the Antonine Wall, where small fortlets were undoubtedly manned by detachments from larger neighbours. Auxiliaries were recruited from amongst those members of the subject-population who were not Roman citizens, and the unit-names – for example, First Cohort of Spaniards – indicate the place of original recruitment. These units were, however, undoubtedly kept up to strength by local recruiting. Their forts made up the policing-network in north-west

Plate 40. Lancaster: rebuilt hypocaust beneath the bath-house.

Plate 41. Brougham: milestone-inscription referring to the CAR[*vetii*] (Brougham Castle Museum). The inscription reads: 'For the Emperor, Caesar Marcus Cassianius Latinius Postumus Augustus, Pious and Fortunate, the *Civitas* of the CAR[*vetii*].

England, and will have been a dominant feature of the Romanised landscape; their needs, both corporately and individually, served to give shape to the local economies of which they provided the focal points.

The auxiliary units were intended to bring diversity to the Roman army, though the general success of Romanisation across the empire meant that they became increasingly similar to the legions. Hadrian introduced a new element of variety into the army by beginning to recruit units of infantry and cavalry of various sizes which we know as 'Irregulars'. These are distinguished from other types of unit by such titles as *pedites* (infantry), *equites* (cavalrymen), *numeri* (detachments), or *cunei* (formations). Little is known of the organisation of these, though some appear to have had specialised skills, such as the 'Numerus Barcariorum' (Detachment of

Bargemen) who served at Lancaster and others are recorded in northern forts in the *Notitia Dignitatum*.[4] They seem to have been housed in existing auxiliary forts, perhaps alongside auxiliary units; one such group was made up of Sarmatian cavalry (from the Danube) who were stationed at Ribchester and were part of a large consignment of such soldiers brought from the Danube following the wars of the emperor, Marcus Aurelius.[5]

All of these troops owed allegiance to the emperor and, through him, to Rome; a group of altars which record the annual oaths of allegiance to Jupiter was found at Maryport, and is now housed in the Senhouse Roman Museum. These altars help to provide

Plate 42. The heavily defended fort at Whitley Castle.

Plate 43. Hardknott: the fort bath-house.

information on the garrison-sequence at Maryport, and some were dedicated by a fort commander, Marcus Maenius Agrippa, who was a friend of the emperor, Hadrian. It is upon such altars and other inscriptions and dedications, upon stamped roofing tiles and occasional references in documents, such as the Vindolanda tablets or discharge certificates (Diplomas) of soldiers, that we are dependent for our knowledge of the disposition and movement of the Roman army in north-west England. Occasionally too finds of metal-work which are characteristic of particular areas of the Empire may offer clues to the nature and identity of units which may have been in garrison at particular forts. For example, finds of eastern European metal-work may provide indications of the disposition of more of Marcus Aurelius' Sarmatian irregulars.

After their periods of service the troops of the army were discharged with land and other bounties: legionaries might receive theirs within the context of a town (*colonia*), though frequently auxiliary and irregular troops probably received theirs in the form of small-holdings close to where they had served. In this way, Julius Januarius, a cavalry NCO ('decurion'), appears to have farmed land at Bolton-le-Sands presumably after seeing service at Lancaster.[6] On a larger scale, veterans appear to have made up a significant settlement around the fort at Ribchester. It may well be that in the organisation of land-ownership and tenure in north-west England, some – perhaps, the best – land was appropriated by the authorities for the purpose of veteran-settlement. Obviously, such settlement will have brought constant diversification into the social and economic faces of north-west England.

It is thus crucial that we do not take a blinkered view of the Roman army as a blunt instrument of oppression; as we shall see, it was far more than this, though our ability to look at the army's role in detail is severely hampered by the patchy and inadequate

Plate 44. Ravenglass: the fort bath-house.

Plate 45. Maiden Castle-on-Stainmore: terraces cut for rectangular buildings.

Plate 46. Manchester: iron-roasting hearth.

nature of the surviving evidence. From the *Antonine Itinerary*,[7] the *Notitia Dignitatum*[8] and the *Ravenna Cosmography*[9] we have

Plate 47. A group of local and imported pottery, Bowness-on-Solway.

documentation of road routes, place names and troop dispositions (See Appendix IV). But very few place-names are independently attested on inscriptions from sites, which means that road-routes and place-names (and therefore unit dispositions) are very difficult to fix. The discovery of new sites and new stretches of roads[10] shows that we cannot yet take for granted the general directions of the Itineraries. Further, the fact that we lack detailed chronologies for most sites means that often we do not know even whether particular sites were under occupation when the routes were drawn up. It is thus possible with many of the routes to propose a number of alternative schemes[11] without even then necessarily approaching certainty.

Again with the *Notitia Dignitatum* which provides a list of sites and military units in the north, we are left with problems of dating and interpretation in the document itself;[12] yet more than this, our lack of knowledge of the place-names allows few positive identifications to be made. In any case few of the inscriptions from the sites themselves, which carry information about garrison-units, can be precisely dated. Thus, too often, although we know that a certain unit was in garrison at a certain site, we cannot tell when, which means in its turn that we lack the essential data to bring clarity to the *Notitia*. It is, however, clear from surviving documents, that units were moved around; for example, the changes of frontier-policy in the second century necessitated much movement. A clear implication of such movements of troops to new bases is that their previous garrison-forts may have been abandoned – even if only temporarily. There is, for example, reasonable evidence to suggest the temporary abandonment of a number of forts in north-west England when Antoninus Pius decided upon the reoccupation of southern Scotland in the 140s.

On the whole, however, we are limited to the most general observations about the garrison-pattern. Following conquest and consolidation the military emphasis clearly moved north in the second century towards the frontiers and their hinterlands. Although the picture is very unclear in the second half of the second century, there must have been renewed attention under Severus and Caracalla in the frontier area, although the successful conclusion of their activities may have allowed a considerable degree of demilitarisation for most of the third century. From the middle of the third century, increasing political instability at the centre meant that troop movements must have been occasioned by the dictates of civil, as well as external, enemies. Britain, for example, was affected by the upheavals of the *Imperium Galliarum* (AD 259–73), in which the western provinces separated from the central government; further disturbance took place in the 280s and 290s when Carausius and Allectus ruled Britain separately, and still more such difficulties occurred in the 340s and 380s. Rebuilding in the early fourth century of a number of forts on Hadrian's Wall suggests a remilitarisation of the frontier, and the evidence indicates the retention of a strong military presence well into the second half of the fourth century.

The paucity of evidence makes it hard to study in detail the political, social, economic and cultural impact of the Roman army in the north-west; the generally accepted picture remains heavily dependent upon information from a relatively small proportion of available sites. As we have seen, initial resistance to the progress of the Roman army was tough, but by no means universal, amongst the Brigantes. Evidence suggests that some hostility at least was still present in the second century; references in Roman writers support it, and we may assume that the complex frontier movements of the second century represented a response to dangers and threats, continuing into the early third century. Precision is

Plate 48. Watercrook: an enamelled brooch.

Plate 49. Head of a bone hair-pin.

harder to achieve: references to 'Brigantian rebellions' in the second century remain elusive, and at least one – that of Pausanias referring to the reign of Antoninus Pius – may not concern Britain at all. However, an indication of disturbed conditions – although probably at a later date – is provided by the tombstone of Flavius Romanus from Ambleside; with a frankness unusual for a tombstone-inscription, Romanus is described as having been killed by the enemy *inside* his fort.[13] Further, we may begin to wonder whether Roman buildings, which are described as having 'collapsed through old age',[14] may in fact have met more violent ends.

Plate 50. Vindolanda: the *mansio*.

Although traditionally we think of the north as 'the military zone', and Roman forts provide a reminder of military imperatives in the area, yet considerable parts of Brigantian territory were apparently handed over to the local people for their administration. In the second century a *civitas* (civil administration) of the Brigantes was established east of the Pennines and centred on the town of Aldborough. Inscriptions from Old Carlisle[15] and Brougham[16] indicate that in the third century the Carvetii, evidently a 'sub-group' of the Brigantes, were also 'promoted' to the status of a *civitas*. The administrative centre was presumably at Carlisle, where excavations have not only indicated the extent of the town, but have also provided evidence for substantial structures, such as a large, hypocausted courtyard house in Keays Lane,[17] other substantial buildings in the Lanes area, and a long-lived strip-house at Blackfriars Street.[18]

Certainly, on present evidence, Carlisle outstrips other north-west 'towns' in its extent and in the scope of its buildings. How large an area was administered by the Carvetii is harder to say, though it has been suggested that the milestone[19] at Middleton-in-Lonsdale, which marks a distance of fifty-three miles from Carlisle, represents the southern boundary of the tribal *territorium*. There may have been other 'sub-groups' similar to the Carvetii, and it has long been held that Ptolemy's *Portus Setantiorum* (The Harbour of the Setantii), was situated at the mouth of the Wyre, and was the centre of tribal territory in the Lancashire Fylde. It has, however, to be said that there is as yet no precise clue to the location of the Setantii (see above in chapter 2).

It is at any rate certain that Roman confidence in 'ceding' administrative responsibilities to the Carvetii[20] points to the existence of a

Plate 51. Vindolanda: strip-building.

class of tribal leaders of sufficient loyalty, wealth and influence to be able and willing to shoulder these responsibilities. In its turn this suggests the development of relationships between local people and Roman administrators, which must have been based on the economic success of local farmers and craftsmen in supplying the needs of the Roman army. It also indicates persuasively that for the most part the relationship that developed between Roman and native was constructive and mutually productive, rather than antagonistic.

Of course, in the early days of occupation the landscape was dominated by the physical signs of conquest and policing – the Roman forts themselves and the roads that linked them. If we can draw analogies from other places, the land between the forts will have become the responsibility of the fort commanders. The manner of its treatment will have depended upon a number of factors. For example, areas which had resources of precious metals will probably have been made into imperial estates, and run either directly by the army or by 'trusted' groups treated as lessees. The heavily-defended fort at Whitley Castle probably exercised such a role in the lead / silver industry. Some land will have been taken over by units of the army and used for its own purposes; for example, as can be seen at Hardknott, a considerable area was required for a parade-ground. Land might be taken over by the army for industrial purposes, and particularly in the vicinity of cavalry-forts, extensive areas of grassland may have been cultivated by the army-units themselves. Again, a 'reserve' of land must have been kept for the settlement of discharged soldiers.

Thus, the presence of units of the Roman army had an inevitable and direct effect on

Plate 52. Maryport: celtic horned god
(copyright, Senhouse Museum Trust).

Plate 53. Carlisle: dedication to Mars Ocelus and
the imperial cult (Carlisle Museum and Art
Gallery). The insription reads: 'to the God, Mars
Ocelus, and to the Divine Spirit of the Emperor
... Augustus'.

Plate 54. Ribchester: dedication to Apollo
Maponus.

landscape-management. However, we should not be misled into seeing this as the 'desolation' attacked so bitterly by Calgacus; the other side of the picture is seen vividly in Dio Cassius' description of the early days of Romanisation in Germany, where the native-population was 'becoming accustomed to hold markets and was meeting in peaceful assemblages'. The Roman army, its needs and infrastructure held clear advantage for people living in the areas which it policed.

The roads themselves, which in the north-west penetrated some very difficult terrain, had advantages for civilians as well as soldiers; the military arterial routes became central features of a growing network of roads which served to link local farmers and industrialists into the Romanised economy.

Finds of Roman material – particularly coins and coin-hoards[21] – demonstrate this point clearly. As we shall see, many farmers were left as landowners or tenants to pursue their traditional trades – but now with large new markets to satisfy. However, those most directly affected by the army's presence were the merchants and craftsmen who followed in its wake, and settled outside the forts forming the small towns referred to as *vici*. Such development usually occurred in ribbon fashion along one or more of a fort's access roads (as at Vindolanda), or may, as at Old Carlisle, have focussed on a nearby main road.

There was apparently no standard size, shape or mode of development attaching to *vici*, though to a degree judgement needs to be suspended in view of the small amount of excavation that has taken place on such sites. Most forts in north-west England supported *vici*; only Hardknott appears not to have done, its small extra-mural bath-house servicing a military community alone. Even at the summit of the Stainmore Pass, terracing to the south of the fort at Maiden Castle represents artificial platforms provided for the construction of rectangular stone buildings. Clearly the size of the *vicus* would depend on the size and importance of its fort; and a legionary fortress such as Chester, with its 5,500 soldiers, would support much more extensive civilian settlement than an auxiliary fort intended for only 500 troops.

Obviously, however, much will have depended on the *importance* of an individual fort. Papcastle,[22] for example, a large fort which probably had a key role in the management of security in the interface between the northern Lake District and the good agricultural land of the Solway Plain, seems to have supported an extensive *vicus*; so too does Ambleside, presumably because of the supply-role deriving from its position at the head of Lake Windermere. Aerial photography suggests that *vici* were not planned homogeneously, but developed as the stimulus to do so occurred. They appear to have lacked the prestigious town-centre administrative buildings familiar in the *civitas* centres of the south – presumably because they did not enjoy any administrative control over their own affairs, but deferred to the fort-commanders.[23] Informal 'associations', however, did occur, as is shown by a dedication to the god, Vulcan, made by the *Vikani* (townspeople) of Vindolanda.[24] Some *vici* appear to have been relatively densely settled, whereas others, generally referred to as 'dispersed *vici*', were rather more like occasional small settlements on the roads leading out of a fort (as at Brougham). It is generally assumed that *vici* did not have defensive walls, although at Ribchester excavation has revealed traces of a defensive rampart and ditch apparently enclosing the settlement. The interpretation of this feature is still unclear, although it is possible that Ribchester may have constituted a 'special case', because of retired soldiers being settled in the *vicus* – as the Roman name BRESNETENACI VETERANORVM - seems to imply.[25]

In many cases, *vici* appear to have begun development very soon after the establishment of a fort;[26] buildings initially, as at Watercrook, were of timber, but were in most cases converted to stone later. Typical of these buildings were long, narrow, structures with their gable-ends facing on to the street. These buildings had internal divisions which may have provided for a shop on the street frontage, with living accommodation behind and perhaps a 'yard' at the rear where the resident family (or families) engaged in producing goods which could be offered for sale in the shop. In most cases access to individual rooms was not provided by an independent corridor but had to be gained by proceeding through one room to another. Only if neighbouring buildings, which would normally be separated by a narrow alley-way, came under single ownership could the alley be roofed to provide an internal corridor.

Inhabitants of such buildings may have been traders or craftsmen attracted over long

Figure 5. Find-spots of Roman coin-hoards.

distances by the market which the fort represented, though most of those who lived in the *vici* were probably more local in origin: many young women, for example, may have been attracted by unofficial liaisons formed with serving soldiers which could be formalised into marriage after a soldier's demobilisation. From the time of Septimius Severus, however, soldiers were allowed to marry whilst still serving.

Although we have little direct evidence of the nature of *vicus*-populations, it appears likely that they were diverse in nature and origin, though linked by their common ability

Plate 55. Papcastle: statuette of Marsyas (photograph, Lancaster University Archaeological Unit.

to provide something which soldiers needed. Undoubtedly, many craftsmen were attracted by the opportunities, and a number of *vici* have provided evidence of industrial activity in the form of furnaces, weaving equipment, kilns, tanning-pits as well as waste products from many processes.[27] Metal-working will obviously have occupied a major place in the industrial life of the *vici* in order to undertake repairs of military and civilian property, and to produce a wide range of tools, utensils, fittings and decorative items. Much of this was probably organised on an individual basis, though the *vicus* which lay to the north of the fort at Manchester[28] had a considerable area devoted to furnaces, housed apparently in sheds and 'lean-to' structures, which might justify its description as an 'industrial estate'. It is not surprising that Vulcan, the patron-deity of metal-workers, is the object of a dedication found in the *vicus* at Vindolanda.

In the early days of the *vici* at least, the military and civilian communities will have depended upon local potters to supplement the supply of vessels which could be acquired from other sources. In some cases, the need for a range of terracotta products – tiles and bricks as well as pottery – was such that military units themselves might in a location adjacent to a good supply of suitable raw materials establish an industrial complex, as happened at Quernmore (near Lancaster). Fine wares, such as the red-glazed samian pottery, were imported from Europe, and were presumably sold by travelling salesmen to local shops for selling-on to individuals. In course of time, the supply of such basic products appears to have been organised on a far larger scale with substantial military contracts beings placed with manufacturers in various parts of the country; for example, the British fine-ware known as 'colour-coated' was manufactured in very large quantities in the Nene Valley; black and grey cooking-pots were made in various centres in southern England. In the north-west, large industrial sites, sufficiently well organised to handle substantial contracts developed at such places as Heronbridge, Stockton Heath and Wilderspool (see below).

There will have been plenty of work for joiners in the *vici*, particularly when many of the buildings will have been constructed of timber, and when much repair work of wooden structures and vehicles will have been necessary. Joiners' tools have often been found, and they of course will have constituted an important product for the metal-worker. Nor should we forget that the timber used by the joiner as his raw material and by other tradesmen for the firing of furnaces presupposes the availability of local supplies which could have been kept up only by a sophisticated programme of woodland management.

This serves to emphasise the relationship between fort and *vicus* on the one hand with the adjacent countryside on the other. In no sense, however, will this relationship have been more crucial, as the Vindolanda writing-tablets indicate, than in the supply of food to the forts and to individual traders. It goes without saying that local farmers will have geared their activities not only to supply their own families and satisfy the taxman, but also to produce a surplus to be sold. Such products must have taken account of the tastes of the market; for example, studies of butchered bones indicate that optimum ages for slaughter were recognised and observed.[29] One site at Vindolanda has been identified as a likely butcher's-shop because of its counter and the provision of an internal drain linked to the main 'sewer' outside in the street.[30] In all, a wide variety of food products was undoubtedly sold in *vicus*-shops, and perhaps in many cases precooked to be sold as 'take-away' meals. Similarly, we may assume that local farmers were well prepared to provide hides and fleeces for the manufacture in the *vici* of shoes and clothes, although in the case of hides some might be taken by the authorities as 'tax' for the manufacture of tents.

Thus, the available evidence points not only to a vibrant trading-situation in the *vici*, but also close relationships between the *vicus*-traders and the wider tribal community. There were, of course, many other services available in the *vici*. We may, for example, with confidence postulate a 'leisure-industry' in the form of bars, restaurants, and brothels. The bath-houses provided, under official auspices, the closest equivalent that the Roman world had to our 'leisure-centres', and often provided both for soldiers and civilians not simply bathing facilities, but also a range of other relaxation-activities. Because of its crowded nature, the bath-house was not just a major social centre, but could also provide 'cover' for criminal activities too. Again, the constant heating of water required in the bath-house emphasises the need for large timber-supplies in the area adjacent to the *vicus*.

Plate 56. Kirkham: three mother-goddesses.

Plate 57. Carrawburgh: mithraeum.

Our knowledge of *vici*, fragmentary though it is, provides evidence of other structures and services. Vindolanda, for example, had a 'hotel' (*mansio*), a large building consisting of rooms arranged around an open courtyard, with its own bath-house and stables. This provided basic accommodation for official travellers, particularly the couriers of the imperial post. It is quite likely that evidence of a small bath-house as part of a large courtyard building recognized to the north of the fort at Lancaster indicates a *mansio* at that site too.

The evidence of surviving inscriptions indicates that a wide variety of religious practices will have been catered for in the *vici* – though not necessarily all contemporaneously. Traditionally, Romans and the Romanised Celtic peoples of the west were superstitious, and looked to divine help and protection in a wide variety of activities.[31]

Because of this, religion had always proved to be a powerful political weapon, since the authorities, in their priestly roles, could advise people on action that needed to be taken to keep the gods happy. In pre-Roman Britain, the force of religion and the power of the priests is amply demonstrated not only by what classical writers have said about the druids, but also – and in a more dramatic fashion – in the north-west by the apparent ritual murder suffered by the Cheshire bog-body known as 'Lindow Man'. In Britain, Roman and Celtic divinities were able to come into close relationship: both communities were polytheistic and both saw their gods as presiding over particular activities. These were often brought together in the so-called *interpretatio Romana*, in which a Roman and equivalent Celtic deity were effectively 'fused' into one – for example, Apollo Maponus at Ribchester,

71

Mars Ocelus at Carlisle, and Mars Cocidius at Bewcastle. It enabled the Roman authorities to cause little disturbance to existing beliefs, except perhaps to organise them in a more formal way. For example, at Carrawburgh (on Hadrian's Wall), where in the pre-Roman period a natural spring was regarded as the manifestation of the goddess, Coventina, the spring was enclosed in a concrete basin and housed in square 'Romano–Celtic' temple. Dedications to Coventina also show how she came to be perceived in anthropomorphic form.

Certain religious observances were required officially. Although most Roman emperors did not view themselves as gods, their extraordinary position in society was marked by the 'imperial cult' in which an obligatory demonstration of political loyalty was channelled through the observance of their 'divine spirit' (numen). Numerous surviving altars and dedications record such statements of loyalty on the parts of units of the Roman army, and of other groups and individuals. As head of the Roman pantheon, Jupiter, the Greatest and Best, (Jupiter Optimus Maximus or IOM), received especial attention as a focus of political interest; individuals might purchase small statuettes of emperors or of official Roman gods to place in their own homes as indications of their own loyalty. Of course, these statuettes, such as the Manchester Jupiter, constituted for metal-workers and potters products for which the market would never dry up.

Particular groups and individuals would see divine associations of particular relevance to themselves; the army, for example, would look to Mars and Hercules, and sometimes brought these to Britain in forms familiar to them in their own countries of origin. Thus, a unit of Germans at Housesteads put up a dedication to Mars Thincsus. Others might equate Mars with a deity native to Britain, such as Mars Cocidius (at Bewcastle). Metal-workers sought the especial protection of the smith-god, Vulcan, whilst musicians might look to Apollo. A dedication-stone from Ribchester to Apollo Maponus portrays the god with his lyre, and an apparent temple-site at Papcastle produced a bronze statuette of the satyr-figure, Marsyas, who was worsted by Apollo in a music-contest, and then flayed alive for his temerity in having issued a challenge to the god of music.

There are also examples of local deities becoming Romanised, but not equated with a Roman god. Thus the spring-goddess, Coventina, presumably guaranteed water-supplies at Carrawburgh, whilst Ialonus (perhaps the deity of the river Lune at Lancaster) was invoked by an ex-soldier, presumably to bring health to his crops. In a similar way, the protection sought for the well-being of a town or tribe could be channelled through a personified tutelary deity; a relief-carving of the goddess Brigantia which was found at Birrens represented the tutelary deity of the Brigantes in the classical form of a winged-victory figure. Similarly a small stone bust from Carlisle, depicted wearing a 'gated' crown, was the tutelary deity of this town of the Carvetii.

In addition to these official and semi-official deities, the forts and vici of the north-west have provided ample evidence of non-Roman 'mystery' cults – such as Sun-worship, Mithraism, Isis-worship and, of course, Christianity. These cults, which, unlike the state cults, were practised in the secrecy of their temple-buildings, mostly originated in the eastern Mediterranean and found their way to Britain through the movements of soldiers and merchants. They became more popular because they offered a hope to the individual of salvation from and a 'personal relationship' with a god, which were not essentially features of the state cults. They were tolerated so long as they did not encourage conflict; the Roman objection to Christianity was based upon the refusal of Christians to render their obligations to the state-cults.

The secrecy attaching to most of these cults

prevents our knowing a great deal about them, and generally they appear to have enjoyed intermittent observance at particular places – presumably because they needed the authority and financial resources of a senior person – (for example, a fort commander) – to lead them. There may also have been an element of fashion and political expediency attaching to such cults, as is presumably the case with the dedication at York early in the third century AD to the Egyptian god, Serapis, at the time when York provided the base for the emperor, Septimius Severus, and his family who were themselves devotees of the cult.

Few temples dedicated to these cults survive: their presence is generally attested by inscriptions or cult-objects. The most tangible evidence is provided by the cult of the Persian god of light, goodness and truth, Mithras, who attracted interest amongst both soldiers and merchants. The best-preserved Mithraic temple in Britain is the small rectangular building situated off the south-west corner of the fort at Carrawburgh. It had four separate periods of use between the mid-second and early fourth centuries when it was finally destroyed violently, probably at the hands of Christians who regarded the Mithraic liturgy as a kind of 'devilish' version of their own. The temple has a central nave, which would have been dominated by the highly colourful relief of Mithras slaying the primeval bull and allowing its blood and semen to soak into the earth and to become the source of life and fertility for mankind. The nave was flanked by 'aisles' on which were situated benches on which initiates could recline during the ritual meal. Separated from this was an ante-chamber where would-be initiates may have been 'tested' before being allowed into the sanctum. It is likely that the atmosphere was 'heady', due to the burning of pine-cones and the very restricted lighting, of which one feature survives – an altar depicting Mithras wearing the sun-ray crown on which the rays have been pierced through so that a light placed at the back of the altar could shine through them.

Although no other Mithraic temples have been found in the north-west (except at Housesteads, also on Hadrian's Wall), various sites have produced Mithraic sculptures – Chester, Manchester, Maryport and possibly Lancaster, too, where one piece in a hoard of sculpture found in the late 18th century has Mithraic features.

The evidence for Christianity in the forts and *vici* of the north-west is less promising than for other religions. Christianity was, until Constantine's Edict of Milan of AD 312, a forbidden religion; this meant that the activities of Christians until then had to be conducted covertly. Even after AD 312, the administrative classes of the empire were slow to renounce traditional paganism. The surviving evidence all consists of individual items, from which generalisations cannot readily be drawn; no Christian structure survives from the late Roman period in the north-west. Yet it is likely that during the fourth century at least there must have been converts, and groups of Christians will have gained in confidence.

The earliest evidence for Christianity in the north-west is provided possibly by a fragment of amphora-wall from the *vicus* at Manchester; this fragment was inscribed with part of a 'word-square', in which the re-arranged letters give the words PATER NOSTER (twice) with two spare As and Os, The words PATER NOSTER of course mean 'Our Father' and the letters of the square allow them to be arranged in a cruciform fashion; the letters 'A' and 'O' are Latin renderings of the Greek letters 'alpha' and 'omega', ('the beginning' and 'the end') which were often used as a Christian cryptogram.[32] The context of the Manchester example is mid-second century AD, although it has to be said that, as with the similar example from Cirencester, not all authorities are agreed that such word-squares do in fact necessarily have a Christian significance.

Three tombstones from the north-west betray indications of Christian burials; two –

Plate 58. Carrawburgh: mithraic altars.

(one each from Carlisle and Brougham)[33] – employ the formula which indicates that the deceased person lived for 'x years *more or less*'. The vagueness was an indication of the relative unimportance of the length of time spent on earth. The third – from Maryport – is a fragment which contains the Christian cryptogram, *chi-rho*, the first letters in Greek of *Christos*.[34] For the rest, personal objects such as lamps and finger-rings are the only indications of Christian owners.

It has been suggested that unusual church-dedications may offer a clue to the locations of early Christian communities: in this case, a dedication to St Elphin – (Romano–British name, Alphinus) – at Warrington may be significant. Beyond this, any pre-conquest Christian evidence may conceal the existence of Romano–British Christian centres. Thus, the church-sites at Heysham Head, Urswick and Aldingham may be of interest in this connection.

A further aspect of Romanised town-life was entertainment and ceremonial. Traditionally, gambling was popular and was undoubtedly carried on widely in bars and on pavements. Evidence of board-games – (possibly of the war-game type) – has been found in the north-west in the shape of a 'board' made of stone, and crudely divided up into squares, and of a large collection of bone counters which was located in a barrack-area at Ravenglass.[35] The stone-built amphitheatre at Chester[36] provides evidence of more organised entertainment and ceremonial. Such sites were obviously relevant in the context of the large military and civilian population to be expected of a legionary fortress, but smaller versions may have been located close to other fort- and *vicus*-sites in the north-west. A pottery face-mask found at Wilderspool[37] may offer a clue to the type of entertainment provided, whilst a vivid indication of military ceremonial is provided by the Ribchester parade-helmet. Because of their size, amphitheatre sites were normally situated at the edges of settlements, as is the case with those at Chester, Caerleon and Cirencester. In some parts of the country – as at Dorchester – there is evidence of the 'conversion' of henge-monuments of suitable size to this purpose.

As we have seen, some of the surviving evidence of Christians in Roman north-west England consists of tombstones which contain the use of formulae of possible Christian significance. Few of the north-west's cemetery sites are known with any certainty. Roman law forbade the placing of any burials (except for those of infants) within settlement areas, and it was normal practice for the roads leading out of towns to be lined with tombs. Thus evidence has come from Penny Street in Lancaster of cremation urns, confirming that that street represents the likely line of a Roman road heading through the *vicus* and continuing along the southern side of the river Lune. Further south, some two miles out of Lancaster (at Burrough Heights), a rectangular earthwork has been located by the side of the Roman road which has been tentatively identified as a substantial roadside-mausoleum.[38] However, the most significant cemetery evidence has come from a site approximately three-quarters of a mile to the south of the fort at Low Borrow Bridge and flanking the eastern side of the road. Evidence has come to light of approximately sixty cremation-urns and a few inhumations, which appear to have been arranged in sub-rectangular or circular plots which were perhaps distinguished by low hedges or fences. One complete tombstone recovered from the site records the death of the age of thirty-five of Aelia Sentica; the stone was erected by her husband, Aurelius Verulus.

The *vicus* provided an incentive for craftsmen to come and set up business: they may even have been officially encouraged to bring themselves within the organised scope of these sites. The *vici* were not, however, the

only sources of manufactured goods available to the north-west's population. Besides the influx of goods from other parts of Britain and even the continent, we have evidence of local industrial sites, some of which were undoubtedly directly controlled by the army.

The most completely known of the military depots in the north-west is the one at Holt in Denbighshire, which serviced the legionary fortress at Chester.[39] The depot was producing tiles and pottery from the late first century into the third, with the peak of activity in the first half of the second. The twenty-acre site produced evidence of 'barracks', a building interpreted as an officer's house, and a bath-house – in addition to the industrial buildings themselves. It is similarly possible that the impressive buildings located at Walton-le-Dale, a site which contains hearths and wells, should also be interpreted as belonging to a legionary depot; the date-range of these, too, appears to be late first to early third century.[40]

Besides these major military depots, smaller (presumably auxiliary) depots have been located: Muncaster presumably supplied Ravenglass and Hardknott,[41] Scalesceugh perhaps Carlisle and Old Penrith; in addition a large tilery was discovered at Brampton;[42] the latter two were operating in the early second century, and should perhaps be connected with the development of the Stanegate *limes*. The Brampton works, which saw the largest examination of all such sites in the north-west, was observed to be of markedly inferior construction compared to the legionary equivalent at Holt. It is thought that in the case of Brampton, the depot was sufficiently close to Old Church fort for the living accommodation to have been provided there. Two further sites of this type, approximately a mile apart, but on the same contour, have been located at Quernmore, some three miles east of Lancaster;[43] at one a crudely constructed tile kiln and a better pottery kiln, together with evidence for iron-working, were located, and thought to fall within the date-range of *c.* AD 80–160. No evidence of administrative buildings was recovered.

Excavations at both Quernmore and Lancaster have put the connection of the two sites beyond question: die-linked stamps of the *Ala Sebosiana* have been recovered at both, and analysis of the clays has confirmed the connection. It should, however, be noted that fragments of hollow voussoir-tiles[44] recovered from the sub-floor debris of the third-century bath-house were found to bear no relationship to the Quernmore material. Since these must post-date the mid-third century rebuilding (*RIB* 605), it confirms the impression that the local tilery was no longer in operation and that supplies must by that time have been organised on a different basis.

The close approximation of dates from sites of this nature suggests that their phasing-out was an act of policy, and presumably reflect two things: first the main phases of building of military sites were complete and repair work would (hopefully) not require building materials on such a scale. Second, larger mass-producing sites elsewhere in the country were presumably by that time (that is, late second / early third centuries) well able to cope with the demands made of them. This is obviously true of pottery, where the bulk of the military market in the later second century was being serviced by east Gaulish samian, black-burnished products from Dorset, and Nene Valley ware.

Industrial activity, mainly iron- and salt-working, has been noted at a number of Cheshire sites: extensive evidence for metal-working, together with a widespread area of sheds and workshops has been revealed at

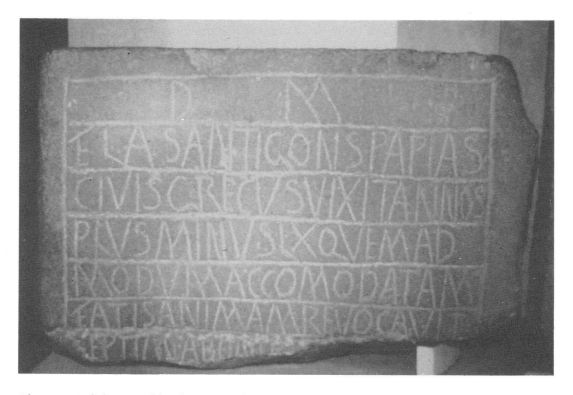

Plate 59. Carlisle: a possibly Christian tombstone (Carlisle Museum and Art Gallery). The inscription reads: 'To the Spirits of the Underworld: Flavius Antigonus Papias, a Greek, lived for sixty years, more or less, and returned to the Fates his soul which had been lent to him for that period of time'.

Figure 6. Rural sites in north-west England.

Heronbridge,[45] ranged on both sides of Watling Street and close by the Dee, a little south of Chester. Activity seems to have continued here from the late first into the third century, although it is not clear whether the site was 'private' or run upon military lines. A similar doubt hangs over Northwich, Middlewich and Whitchurch, all of which have yielded abundant evidence of industrial activity. Conceivably this originated in the context of a *vicus*, since all three sites had military phases. It may well be, however, that when military occupation came to an end, the industrial activity, presumably in the hands of civilians, was able to continue.[46]

Finally, at the point where the road from Northwich to Walton-le-Dale crosses the Mersey, is situated the most extensive of the north-west's industrial sites – at Wilderspool and Stockton Heath. The site, which apparently, as at Heronbridge, straddles the road, has seen a number of extensive excavations,[47] the largest being at the turn of the present century. Many different industrial activities have been recognised – working in iron, bronze and lead, pottery, tile- and glass-making, as well as enamelling.

The site is criss-crossed with fence-posts and ditches, which are presumably property demarcations, though the latter could conceivably be water-channels. A few stone buildings have been located, but the majority are of timber construction; whilst most are basically rectilinear, a circular one located in the excavations of 1976 gives rise to speculation about the nature of the inhabitants. Such a building strongly suggests a native British origin, and it has been suggested that the 'trade-mark' type of *mortarium*-stamp might in fact simply represent illiterate blundering, rather as occurs on copies of Roman third-century radiate coins.

The products of the Wilderspool pottery-kilns have been traced in many parts of the north-west, and as far north as the Antonine Wall. Although a putative set of 'defences' has often been assumed to represent the remains of an Agricolan fort, neither the nature of these features nor the dating-evidence recovered from the site is in fact consistent with such an assumption. Indeed, in common with other 'industrial' sites, occupation appears to have been principally from the end of the first century AD until early in the third, although a scatter of later material[48] indicates that some form of activity continued at Wilderspool into the fourth century. There is also evidence from Wigan which would appear to be consistent with a site of an industrial nature.[49]

The nature of sites like Wilderspool, Heronbridge and the industrial areas of the *vici* suggests that the workers were principally native craftsmen who for one reason or another (voluntarily or under persuasion) came into the organised areas to work – perhaps to secure a better hold on the assured markets which the Roman occupation offered.

The bulk of the population, we can assume, remained as they had long been – arable farmers and pastoralists. However, the lack of excavation of rural sites in north-west England leaves much doubt as to the nature of the relationship between farmers and the populations of the forts and *vici*. There are, in fact, many questions about the nature of the rural economy to which the answers in the present state of our knowledge can be no more than provisional.

Outwardly, the most striking difference between the rural economies of the highland and lowland zones is the absence from the former of structures which are classified as *villas*. The villa estate of the lowland zone represented a level of *architectural* Romanisation in the countryside, and existed alongside rural sites whose nature and appearance are much closer to those found in the north-west; the villa-estate also assumes a certain level of affluence in terms of land and finance.[50] It is clearly too crude an assumption to argue that because the north-west generally lacked villa-estates, its farmers also lacked land and finance, for the establishment of the *civitas* of the Carvetii in northern Cumbria clearly does assume a strong level of wealth amongst its leaders; it is difficult to imagine a source of that wealth other than agriculture.

The north-west has so far yielded two sites which conform to the description of a villa as measured by the criteria used in the lowland zone – Eaton-by-Tarporley (near Chester) and Kirk Sink (near Skipton).[51] There may of course be more to locate, but such a small number may be explained by the movement of a small number of individuals from further south. The vast majority of rural sites in the north-west are made up of circular and sub-rectangular structures in complexes of varying size and constructed either of stone or of timber. Clearly, such complexes consist of both domestic sites and fields or yards. Our knowledge of the distribution of such sites suggests that some were small farms whilst others may well have been the centres of estates of considerable size.

Such study as has taken place indicates that we cannot employ simple criteria such as chronological development or level of Romanisation to explain the differences in shape and building materials. Indeed, artefactual evidence indicates no obvious distinctions in date or ownership, whilst the difference in building materials appears to represent the use of timber on sites located in the valleys with stone used mainly on sites at higher altitude, as at Maiden Castle-on-Stainmore. This in its turn probably does no more than reflect the process (human and environmental) of deforestation. It is clear too that some of least of the rural sites of all types enjoyed long histories. stretching back beyond the Romano–British period (as at Ewe Close in the upper Lune valley or Urswick 'stone walls') and continuing much later (as at Gauber High Pasture in upper Ribblesdale).

There can be no doubt that the presence of the Roman army with its dependent populations in the *vici* will have opened up considerable opportunities for those involved

Plate 60. Chester: the amphitheatre.

in agriculture – tastes in food and drink to be accommodated, as well as openings into the 'textile market', and the provision of hides for tents and for transforming into leather goods, and the rearing of working-animals and fodder for them.

As well as this, whilst most metal and mineral resources will have been officially handled, some scope was probably left for local extraction and profit. Some of these products will have been taken by way of taxation, but farmers and landowners in the north-west will have been left sufficient for their own needs, and many will have had a surplus which could be sold for profit. It is a reasonable assumption that most of those involved in the rural economy will soon have come to appreciate what the market required; as we have noticed already, it is clear that animals reared for meat will have been slaughtered at an 'optimum age'.

How the land was distributed must remain a matter for conjecture, but some must have been appropriated by the authorities for the settlement of discharged soldiers, and it may be assumed that this was likely to have been the land of better quality, such as was situated in coastal areas and in the valley floors. Although the evidence remains inconclusive, it was long ago conjectured that land on the Fylde may have been used for veteran settlement, and it is highly likely that the

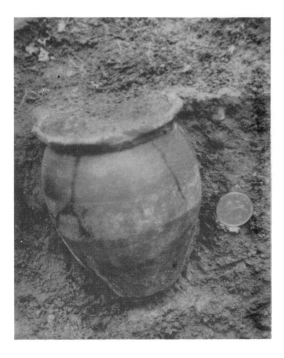

Plate 61. Low Barrow Bridge: cremation-burial (photograph, Lancaster University Archaeological Unit).

veterans of Ribchester, as well as enjoying a stake in the *vicus*, had allotments of land in the Ribble valley. One piece of evidence which may be significant is the altar set up near Bolton-le-Sands by Julius Januarius who described himself as a retired decurion – presumably from the fort at Lancaster. Preferential treatment in the quantity and quality of land distributed will have been afforded to veterans of the legions, of auxiliary cavalry units, and of auxiliary infantry in descending order. It has been suggested that land designated for such use might show signs of centuriation,[52] the traditional Roman form of land-distribution, though at present no certain evidence of this practice has been located.

Despite such imperatives, however, it is unlikely that the authorities were insensitive to the needs and aspirations of Brigantian farmers. Thus much land-tenure and usage was probably left without interference, for it

was by the middle of the first century AD generally held by the Roman emperor and his advisers that local populations were generally easier to manage if left to pursue traditional activities and methods. Also, it can be shown that the belief existed that native populations could advance themselves socially and politically if the profitability of their activities was encouraged. Although the period of Roman occupation may not have led to striking advances in agricultural technology, and although uncontrolled deforestation could obviously not be allowed, the clearance of some land will have greatly enhanced the opportunities for profit-making.

Two factors have been amply demonstrated: first, we clearly have to reject the notion, often advanced in the past, that apart from the areas of the Roman sites themselves, the population of the north-west was thin.[53] Secondly, it is clear from the locations of agricultural sites that there must have been a strong economic inter-dependence between the Roman and native populations, a point also effectively confirmed by the 'stores-lists' preserved in the Vindolanda tablets.[54]

The plotting of sites has proceeded much further in Cumbria than in Lancashire; conditions in the latter do not readily lend themselves to aerial research;[55] thus the number of known sites is small, although finds of Roman material suggest that the Roman roads and the river valleys will have provided the chief foci for settlement. Nonetheless, possible traces of the Romano–British landscape have been observed on the eastern flank of the West Lancashire mosses; and there are signs that the higher ground in the Fylde may have supported settlement.[56]

North of Lancashire, considerable settlement has been observed on the limestone of the Ribblehead area, as at Gauber High Pasture and Colt Park.[57] In north Lancashire and Cumbria, the principal areas of settlement are located in the valley floors and slopes of the communications corridors provided by the Lune and Eden rivers, and again on the

Plate 62. Walton-le-Dale: remains of sheds.

Solway Plain and the northern slopes of the Lake District.[58]

Although excavation of rural sites has been very limited, it would appear a reasonable assumption that a high proportion of them, even if multi-period, was active in the Roman period. It is similarly reasonable to suppose that many, if not most, of the sites, both arable and pastoral, enjoyed an 'economic relationship' with the Roman forts and *vici*. In other words, they were producing grain surplus to their taxation requirement, and their animal husbandry was to an extent organised to take account of the Roman market for meat.[59]

Environmental characteristics were clearly the chief limiting factors to the farmer's activity; in particular, deforestation and soil erosion will have limited the use to which the higher terrain – that is above approximately 350 metres – could be put. At the same time the very process of soil erosion from higher levels will have led to enhanced fertility in the valleys. During the Roman period, deforestation by environmental causes was intensified by the need for timber for building, though in a number of places excavation has revealed that Roman forts were being built in areas already without forest cover, having been given over to grassland or occasionally to ploughing. Deforestation will have affected not only the local farmer's use of the land, but also the materials he used to provide housing for himself. Clearly, stone would have had to be used where timber was in short supply. Thus, for that reason, if for no other, the higher rural settlements would tend to be stone-built – and, incidentally, more resilient to the passage of time. Timber, wattle and thatch were generally used at lower levels, though a circular hut at Fingland appears to have been constructed of turves laid on a stone foundation.[60]

81

A total picture is, of course, beyond recovery; particularly in the valley floors and on the lower slopes subsequent agricultural activity has destroyed a good deal of the evidence. However, the density of sites located, particularly on the good land of the valley floors, suggests a picture of intense agricultural activity, based upon a mixed arable / pastoral economy. Evidence accumulated from the Eller Beck sites in the Lune Valley[61] suggests an extensive system of 'celtic' fields, spreading up the valley slopes and perhaps centred on the valley floor. The presence of 'mixed-farming' sites on the fells (for example, Waitby, Crosby Ravensworth and Crosby Garrett) perhaps indicates an attempt to utilise the slopes in a manner similar to that of the valleys themselves with cultivation carried probably to a higher altitude than nowadays.[62] On the whole, however, the higher-level sites (that is, above approximately 275 metres) carry, in the evidence of dykes and large 'fields', the indications of stock-management and postoralism.[63] In the case of Eller Beck and Waitby, it has been shown that in the later Roman period there is evidence of arable land giving way to a pastoral use.[64] Such distinctions will obviously have been influenced by local environmental circumstances and by changing economic conditions.

As we have seen, rural settlement is identified in generally separate (if not isolated) forms – either rectilinear (as at Cantsfield near the confluence of the Lune and the Greta) or curvilinear (as at Wolsty Hall on the Solway Plain).[65] Most appear to be best described as single farmsteads rather than grouped as 'villages',[66] and generally display single entrances. Rectilinear and curvilinear forms appear to exist contemporaneously, although the rectilinear forms may be more commonly associated with field-systems. They are generally wholly enclosed, presumably to exclude marauders – human or animal – although some, as at Crosby Ravensworth, are partly unenclosed.

Whilst finds of artefacts (in addition to typological analysis) will permit relatively easy recognition of sites which belong to the Romano–British period, the paucity of these artefacts usually precludes close dating. It is generally held that the more settled conditions which prevailed from the late second / early third centuries provided a major stimulus to settlement expansion, although some sites are undoubtedly earlier than this. Expansion includes not just the appearance of new sites, but also the development of existing ones, as happened at Cross Hill[67] (Penrith), where a circular house gave way to rectangular buildings; such a development could suggest the influence of the *vicus* building-types, and thus carry chronological and cultural implications. Care needs, however, to be taken as change over a long period may be involved; for example, at Gauber High Pasture (in upper Ribblesdale),[68] excavation demonstrated that a rectilinear building on a Roman–British site was in fact of ninth century date. Conversely, excavations at Fingland showed clear evidence of a circular structure associated with late Roman pottery.[69] Whilst the huts might be placed anywhere within the enclosures, a striking phenomemon is found at Castle Folds on Orton Scar,[70] where a defensive stone wall-circuit has circular and rectilinear buildings constructed against its interior face.

The usage of rural sites has again to be generally inferred from the few examples which have been the subject of study. It is self-evident that economic advantage will have lain behind a great deal that was done; the realisation of such advantage might range from the position of a farm close to the Romano–British communications and site network to the co-operative management of land which may be visible in the larger field systems. The positioning of many sites tends to indicate that they were intended to take advantage of lower land for arable purposes and higher land for stock-management. Such arable usage would presumably include the growing of crops for sale and for winter-feed

Plate 63. Wilderspool: property-divisions and circular hut.

Plate 64. Colt Park: circular hut and field-walls.

Plate 65. Cantsfield: sub-rectangular farm-structure.

for the stock. The smaller fields intended for arable usage were probably demarcated with low stone banks, whilst larger fields associated with higher turf banks were presumably intended for stock-management.

We can therefore see that in general cereal and hay cultivation took place in ploughed land in the valleys and the lower slopes, whilst grazing for animals was provided on the higher slopes, presumably utilising different areas according to season. It should also be noticed that land-use was not necessarily static; the Eller Beck complex has shown arable land given over to pastoral use in the later Roman period. Some field systems, however, may always have been intended for pastoral use, as at Aughertree Fell on the northern slopes of the Lake District, or at Stone Carr (Penrith) where fields were bounded by deep ditches. Whilst much of the pastoralism was concerned with cattle and the many uses to which they could be put, we should not forget the role of sheep beyond the provision of food. Finds of textiles at Vindolanda demonstrate the potential significance of sheep-farming and the local processing of the wool. There is no reason to suppose that this may not have been carried out by local farmers, producing amongst other things the rather shapeless garments in which the 'cloaked deities' from Housesteads are

depicted – possibly the *birrus britannicus* of Diocletian's Price Edict.

Whilst crop-growing and stock-management provided a living for a large section of the rural community, it should be noticed that for some hunting must have remained more of a living than a pastime. Areas of woodland will have provided a habitat for red deer and wild boar, which could clearly have made an economic contribution.

In short, whilst it has to be said that our knowledge is very selective, it is becoming possible to see a degee of integration between Roman and native in the north-west, which exists on the economic, social and religious levels.[71] The evidence will be seen principally within the urban context, and in the rural

83

environment in the close vicinity of fort / *vicus* sites. The wider rural community will have generated what was required in taxation, and in some cases, a surplus for sale. However, that the volume of that surplus never reached major proportions in the north-west is clear from the general inability of the *vici* to prosper without active support from a military presence. In this sense, Romanisation in the north-west may have advanced – no doubt more for some than others – but it did not attain the level of urbanisation and wealth-creation that we see further south.

Clearly there is much research to be done, particularly on the detailed nature of the economic basis of the sites. Whilst aerial survey and field-work will continue to advance the picture, the excavation of more sites is clearly required. It is, however, possible with the present state of the evidence to see in part the relationship between the Roman troops and the native population – whether as craftsmen or farmers. To a degree, all were harmonised into a Romano–British economy; the native population was producing goods, manufactured or agricultural, on a commercial as well as a taxation basis, for this will explain the presence of items like samian pottery on native sites, which must have been acquired in return for goods.

In short, therefore, it would appear to be far from the truth to argue for a 'conquerors and vanquished' type of relationship in the north-west. The Romans were a stimulus; within limits the local population became Romanised. Whilst progress was less marked and dramatic than in lowland Britain, it would still be reasonable to assert that Roman and native lived together to mutual advantage.

Footnotes – Chapter 6

1. Strabo IV.5.2.
2. *Life of Agricola* 30, 5.
3. For all questions relating to the Roman army, see Webster, 1970.
4. *RIB* 601; Shotter, 1973b.
5. Dio Cassius LXXII.16.
6. *RIB* 600.
7. Rivet, 1970.
8. Ward, 1973; Hassall, 1976
9. Richmond and Crawford, 1949.
10. E.g. Richardson G. G. S. and Richardson A., 1980.
11. See my discussions in Potter, 1979 and Jones and Shotter, 1988.
12. Hassall, 1976; Cf. Richmond, 1935 and Heurgon, 1951.
13. See above on p. 53.
14. E.g. the bath-house and *basilica* at Lancaster (*RIB* 605) which were rebuilt in the 260s.
15. *RIB* 933.
16. *JRS* LV (1965), 224; the inscription is of mid-third-century date.
17. *Britannia* XII (1981), 325f. and XIII (1982), 343f.
18. McCarthy, 1990.
19. Birley E. B., 1953; Potter, 1979, 195 (the milestone is recorded as *RIB* 2283). The possibility of other *civitates* in the north is explored by Jones R. F. J., 1981, who mentions Kirkby Thore as a possible centre.
20. Jones and Higham, 1985.
21. Shotter, 1990.
22. *Britannia* XVI (1985), 276.
23. Salway (1980) suggests the possible sharing of responsibility between the fort-commander and the nearest civilian authority – a suggestion based upon the Roman jurist, Ulpian (*Digest* 50.1, 30)
24. *RIB* 1700 (Cf. *RIB* 899 from Old Carlisle).
25. The name is given in the *Ravenna Cosmography* as BRESNETENACI VETERANORUM; for a discussion see Richmond, 1945.
26. Potter, 1979, 187 (Watercrook).
27. Tylecote, 1962, 222ff.
28. Jones, 1974.
29. Jones G. D. B., 1975.
30. Birley R. N., 1977.
31. Henig, 1984.
32. *Britannia* X (1979), 353.
33. *RIB* 787 (Brougham); *RIB* 955 (Carlisle).
34. *RIB* 856.
35. Potter, 1979, 79ff.
36. Thompson, 1976.
37. Thompson, 1965, 84.
38. Edwards, 1971.

39. Grimes, 1930; Thompson, 1965, 53ff.
40. *Britannia* XIII (1982), 352.
41. Bellhouse, 1960b.
42. Hogg, 1965.
43. Jones and Shotter, 1988.
44. Shotter, 1983.
45. Thompson, 1965, 60ff.
46. Jones, 1974, 147f.
47. Thompson, 1965, 67ff.; Hinchcliffe and Williams, 1992.
48. Webster, 1975.
49. *Britannia* XV (1984), 286.
50. Branigan, 1980.
51. For Kirk Sink, see *Britannia* V (1974), 416 and VI (1975), 238; for Eaton-by-Tarporley, see *Britannia* XIII (1982), 353.
52. E.g. Richardson A. (1982), for the discussion of an area near Old Penrith.
53. See now the distribution map in Higham, 1980, 42.
54. Bowman and Thomas, 1983.
55. Higham and Jones, 1975;
56. Jones G. D. B., 1979, 79ff.; for a site at Salford, see *Britannia* XX (1989), 281.
57. *YAJ* XLI 1966, 559–60; King, 1978.
58. Higham and Jones, 1975; Higham, 1978; 1979; 1980; 1982.
59. Jones G. D. B., 1975; Bowman and Thomas, 1983; Davies, 1971; Manning, 1975.
60. Richardson G. G. S., 1977, 57.
61. Lowndes, 1963 and 1964; Higham, 1979.
62. Pennington, 1970.
63. E.g. Aughertree Fell (Bellhouse, 1967).
64. Higham and Jones, 1975, 40ff; Higham, 1979, 34.
65. Blake, 1959, 7ff.
66. Higham, 1980, 41.
67. *Britannia* VIII (1977), 377.
68. King, 1978.
69. Richardson G. G. S., 1977.
70. Richmond, 1933; Higham, 1979.
71. Manning, 1975.

7. The Later Years

We have seen that Severus by armed force and then his son Caracalla by diplomacy appear to have secured with the Scottish tribes some kind of agreement which apparently brought a large measure of peace to the north for a good deal of the third century. It is less clear, however, how far the military grip was relaxed: a major problem in the approach to this question lies in the nature of the evidence: in general, the pottery is less clearly dated for the third and fourth centuries than it is for the first and second. Further, coin-loss evidence is also less reliable for the period, being complicated by the monetary crises that deepened as the third century wore on, and by the *annona militaris* – the practice of paying troops at least partly in kind, which started late in the century.

It is certain that (with the exception of the forts) the Cumberland coast defences, which had been abandoned late in the second century, were not in use during the third – although, as we shall see, there *is* evidence which suggests a selective reactivation in the fourth. Building-inscriptions and other evidence of building-activity indicate that some forts were certainly being kept in repair in the first half of the third century (for example, at Ribchester, Manchester, Lancaster, Watercrook, Old Carlisle, Old Penrith).[1] The second half of the century, however, presents a more confused picture.

In the first place, the civilian authority that was in being by the 260s in the form of the *Civitas Carvetiorum* implies internal peace in the north-west and perhaps a desire to place more of the burden of administration on to the local population. It is likely, too, that Hadrian's Wall, much of which was rebuilt in

the Severan period, was left free from enemy-attack during this period: the result was probably that garrisons were reduced or even removed, as certainly happened at Watercrook, where a fresh coin of AD 320 in the top of the ditch-fill implies demilitarisation by that stage. There is evidence to suggest that some Hadrian's Wall forts (for example, Castlesteads, Birdoswald, Halton Chesters, Rudchester and Wallsend) and the wall itself fell into a state of considerable disrepair. It is possible that these sites were not actually abandoned, but held by token numbers: it has been suggested that the new, smaller, type of barrack-block shown to have been built at Housesteads, Birdoswald and other wall forts in the early fourth century implies a reduced and perhaps less well organised garrison, or perhaps a population of both military personnel and civilians.

Secondly, changes in the nature of the army command-structure, where unit commanders were much more likely to have been soldiers risen from the ranks than the men of higher social status that had been usual before, may have meant a loss of discipline. Further, fewer of the troops were now formed into regular auxiliary units, and more reliance was placed on the units of irregulars. Internally, therefore, peaceful conditions together with the contemporary state of the army itself seem to have combined to produce a relaxed, if not lax, holding of the north-west in the later third century.

If the province was not troubled with anxieties on its northern frontier, there were certainly problems elsewhere, which will have had their effect in the north. Inflation ran wild in the middle of the third century – at least partly due to the fact that successive emperors in their efforts to maintain their positions 'printed money' in order to hand out as bribes funds they did not possess. The resultant chaos is evidenced by the large number of 'radiate copies', often of very poor standard, which were in circulation; there were clearly a number of copying centres for these in the north including (probably) Brougham and Carlisle. Further, attempts made by emperors between *c.* AD 270 and 300 to remove this 'bad money' seem in the case of Britain to have largely failed. The demoralising effect of economic chaos can be paralleled from more recent history.

Again, Severus' reforms of the army and its command-structure, which led to promotion through the ranks to senior army commands – and higher – had the effect by the middle of the century of making anarchy virtually endemic in the empire. It led not only to a constant stream of 'pretenders', but eventually to breakaway movements such as the independent Empire of the Gauls (*Imperium Galliarum*) in which between AD 259 and 273 the Germanies, Gaul and Britain completely severed their connection with the central government and its officials. How far (if at all) this led to the removal of troops from Britain is unclear. The British army's loyalty to the new rulers is evidenced by such inscriptions as the Lancaster bath-house stone,[2] from which the name of Postumus, the creator of the *Imperium Galliarum*, was subsequently removed (that is, after AD 273).

Although this rebellion collapsed in AD 273, to be followed by a series of rather stronger central government emperors, the eventual 'solution', enacted by Diocletian, was the establishment of first a dyarchy, and a little later, a tetrarchy which consisted of two senior figures (*Augusti*) and two junior (*Caesares*), each of whom was responsible for a section of imperial territory. However, in Britain, Carausius, who had been appointed by Maximian (Diocletian's fellow-*Augustus*), to keep the English Channel and the North Sea free of pirates, decided that the principle of split power could be extended: he minted a coin with three obverse heads (his own, Diocletian's and Maximian's)with the legend CARAVSIVS ET FRATRES SVI (Carausius and his brothers). Since Diocletian and Maximian failed to regard Carausius as their brother, his position in AD 287 became *ipso facto* rebellious. Carausius maintained himself until AD 293, when he was murdered by his associate, Allectus, who survived until ousted three years later by the central government in the person of Constantius Chlorus, who was 'Caesar' in the west.

The details of the rebellion do not concern us except in so far as it was a period when attention was paid to the problems of coastal defence. Although not of uniform date, the Saxon-Shore fort system in the south-east owed a good deal of its impetus to this period, and Allectus' 'Galley' coin-reverses stress a similar preoccupation. The new forts were architecturally very different from their predecessors, particularly with their artillery bastions, and indicate a transition in Roman tactical thinking from the 'police station' to the 'defended strong-point'.

The effect of Allectus' attempts to hold his rebel island against the tetrarchs has long been thought to have been a denuding of northern garrisons, leading to an attack on the frontier from the north. There is evidence for both delapidation and demolition in the north in the late third century, and for fire damage at Ravenglass. An inscription records Constantius' involvement in rebuilding at Birdoswald, and other forts of Hadrian's Wall and the hinterland certainly saw reconstruction in the early fourth century.[3] But no evidence points unequivocally to enemy attack at that time.

Constantius was in Britain on at least two occasions – in 296 to crush the rebellion of Carausius and Allectus, and again campaigning in the north in 305–6 against the Picts, and it may well have been in the course of this second visit that he set in train the rebuilding-programme of forts in the north –

Figure 7. Sites occupied after AD 367.

Plate 66. Brougham: hoard of radiate copies of poor quality (Carlisle Museum and Art Gallery).

not only on Hadrian's Wall, but also at sites like Bainbridge and other Pennine forts. Recent work at Housesteads has demonstrated that the third-century barrack-block in the fort's north-east corner had probably decayed, and was replaced early in the fourth century by a far less formal unit consisting of 'chalets' of variable size which were probably stone-built only to half-height. There is similar evidence at Birdoswald of 'chalet-style' buildings replacing earlier barracks; and a contemporary aisled building may be a *basilica equestris exercitatoria* (cavalry drill-hall) attached to the headquarters.[4] The new type of barracks is presumably to be taken as indicating a different type of usage from that for which the building's predecessor was intended – either a combined military and civilian purpose, or army units of a different type, although this is left in doubt by the 'wall sub-section' in the *Notitia* and difficulties surrounding its date of reference (third or fourth century); the sub-section lists the wall forts as garrisoned by the same units as are known from third-century inscriptions, which has led to the suggestion[5] that the chronological reference of this section may in fact be third and not fourth century.

It may be that Constantius' view of and presence in Britain brought about a radical 're-think' of tactics to face the new enemy – the Picts; the post of *Dux Britanniarum* (the northern military commander) was probably created at this time. Further, the rebuilding noted at hinterland forts may suggest that the notion of 'defence in depth' was coming to supersede the idea of the wall as a 'curtain-barrier'. Indeed, the wall itself, as distinct from its forts, may have been less important in the fourth-century arrangements.[6] Thus the post of *Dux Britanniarum* was now added to that of *Comes Litoris Saxonici*, and the pair led the two fourth-century 'frontier' armies in Britain: these armies were distinct from the 'field army' which the emperors took on campaign

Plate 67. Housesteads: 'chalet'-barracks.

with them. In AD 315, Constantine took the title of *Britannicus Maximus*; a particular point of reference is not known, though it may have had some relation to the west coast,[7] or possibly to a continued attention to in-depth readiness, for which Constantine was in fact criticised in antiquity.[8] Possibly we should date the establishment of the west-coast 'Saxon-shore' forts to this period, although reliable dates are not to hand for Cardiff, Caernarvon or Caer Gybi, and the new fort at Lancaster would appear to be a decade or so later than this.

It is difficult to say how far (if at all) a *coherent* west-coast defence system existed. That the Bristol Channel was a significant base at least later in the century seems to be suggested by the letters PR REL (*Praefectus reliquationis classis*) found on a mosaic in the Nodons-temple at Lydney. This, together with the forts at Cardiff, Caernarvon and Caer

Gybi, stresses the importance and vulnerability of the Welsh coasts; it is further likely that a fleet-base in the Bristol Channel will have rendered redundant the legionary fortress at Caerleon (which does not appear to have outlasted the third century). The Bristol Channel base will have linked to the still-maintained legionary fortress at Chester, on the Dee estuary, and thence to Lancaster on the Lune estuary, where probably about AD 330–40 an approximately nine-acre enclosure with polygonal corner-bastions was built on a different alignment from earlier forts. Excavations[9] have also suggested the abandonment of *vicus*-buildings in Lancaster at about this time. It may be significant that Cockersands Moss, just south of Lancaster, was the find-spot of two Nodons statuettes (now lost), thus providing a possible link with Lydney and the Bristol Channel.[10]

In what must have been an increasingly

unstable situation, it is unclear how long life could have been maintained at a reasonable standard in the largely undefended *vici*. Obviously, the length of life of a *vicus* will have represented a response to local conditions, and there is no general date in the north-west that can be applied to the closure of *vici*. At Ribchester, for example, changing environmental conditions may have forced the closure of parts of the *vicus* as early as the later second century. Recent excavations at Lancaster have suggested that *vicus* buildings may have been in the process of abandonment towards the middle of the fourth century, and this may have coincided with the building of the new 'Saxon-shore' type of fort on Castle Hill, which is dated to *c.* AD 330–40. Although the interior structures of most forts in the fourth century are ill-known, it may well be, as we have seen, that what is known would have been consistent with occupation by a population made up of soldiers and civilians. In this case, the forts would have been becoming more akin to 'fortified villages'.

We may assume that in a fast-changing situation, flexibility was a key word: Vegetius describes camouflaged scout-ships (*pictae*) which were used in the fourth century; Lancaster and Morecambe Bay may have seen novel use made of the soldiers of a *Numerus Barcariorum*,[11] whose normal function will have been lighterage.

Arrangements further north on the coast are not easy to describe precisely: the coastal forts of Ravenglass, Moresby, Maryport and Beckfoot were all occupied in the fourth century, although in the cases of Moresby and Beckfoot it is not clear how long that occupation was sustained. Burrow Walls[12] has produced little other than fourth-century pottery, and may well have been a new – or at least very substantially remodelled – fort of the period. There appears also to have been fourth-century reoccupation of some of the long-abandoned sites of the coastal system; at Cardurnock (MF 5),[13] for example, pottery suggested occupation both before and after

AD 367, although the absence of such material at Biglands (MF1) and Swarthy Hill (MF 21) is sufficient to warn us that this was not a full-scale recommissioning.

The context for some of this work may well have been the visit to Britain in the winter of AD 342–3 of the emperor, Constans. The mere fact that the visit was made in the winter is sufficient to indicate that it must have been connected with some emergency, and not just routine in nature. It is known that Constans' visit was in part at least concerned with the *areani* or undercover agents; trouble with them certainly implies disturbance on the northern frontier.

The state of Britain at this time clearly should not be divorced from imperial politics: Constantine's death in 337 had left the Roman world divided between his three surviving sons, Constantine II, Constans and Constantius II. Britain had come within the responsibility of Constantine II, but he was killed in Italy in conflict with Constans in 340. Problems arising out of possible troop-withdrawals from Britain by Constantine II and out of possible disaffection in Britain following upon Constantine II's death may have left a situation uncertain enough to encourage Britain's enemies to take advantage – which may well have been the situation with which Constans intended to deal.

The death of Constans in 350 at the hands of a group who proclaimed Magnentius as his successor also suggests a continuing disturbance in Britain: for evidence such as the frequency of his coins suggests that Magnentius had particular strength in Britain. It is also likely that he again weakened the provinces' military potential by taking troops to Europe to assert his cause. Magnentius' final defeat at the hands of Constantius II in 353 will have brought still further demoralisation to Britain in its wake – first, two further defeats to add to that in which Constantine II had been killed, and second, a witch-hunt in the province following upon Constantius' reassertion of authority.[14]

Plate 68. Lancaster: remains of a fourth-century bastion (the 'Wery Wall').

Plate 69. Caer Gybi: fort-wall and bastion.

In 355 Constantius appointed as western 'Caesar' his cousin, Julian. Although Julian's period showed in a sense the strength of Britain in that in 359 it was possible to use the provinces as a supply-base for his efforts to re-establish the Rhine-frontier, yet less than two years later the continuing insecurity manifested itself in trouble with the Picts and Scotti (from Ireland), which necessitated the posting to Britain of Lupicinus, a very senior officer, with crack units of the 'field army'. The situation remained tense until it came to a head with the 'Barbarian Conspiracy'[15] in 367, in which all of the enemies of Roman Britain appear to have attacked at once. Such an apparently unlikely event as a 'conspiracy' is made perhaps less unlikely when it is realised how deep was the involvement of Romanised 'barbarians' in Roman political and military affairs. It is possible that leaked information about the contemporary difficulties of the emperor Valentinian I was the trigger for this action:[16] the opportunity was evidently enhanced by the treacherous activities of the *areani*[17] who were disbanded in the wake of the catastrophe.

Valentinian's response was to send to Britain, again with a crack 'field army', Theodosius, the father of the later emperor Theodosius. Ammianus makes it clear that the situation – military, urban and rural – was one of almost total disarray. We should, however, beware of assuming that every *archaeological* sign of trouble relates to this particular year: as we have seen, 367 had been the climax of nearly two and a half decades of uncertainty and raiding. Theodosius' achievement was considerable – restabilisation of the military situation, the rebuilding of forts and towns, and the restoration of rural peace.

That the majority of north-western sites either survived the barbarian attack or were rebuilt and occupied after, is clear from the ubiquity of the calcite-gritted wares that were the characteristic product of the Crambeck potteries of east Yorkshire in the second half of the fourth century. Similarly, the absence of this type of pottery provides a good indicator of forts that were probably not included in the restoration. It would certainly appear that there was no attempt to recover forts to the north of Hadrian's Wall, and doubt hangs over the continued use of some forts to the south of it (for example, Ribchester and Watercrook), though it has to be stressed in the consideration of this question, as with others, that a number of the forts have as yet no evidence upon which a statement about their occupation at this stage could be based.

Forts in the north-west which were reconstructed in this period show no sign of the 'Saxon-shore' architecture that had been

Plate 70. Birdoswald: blocking of east gateway.

impenetrability which was a feature of the 'Saxon-shore' forts. At both Ravenglass and Bowness-on-Solway[18] excavation has shown that a new constructional technique for internal buildings was employed in this final phase. Instead of foundation beams, buildings were apparently supported on a 'frame' of heavily packed posts.

Reconstruction is everywhere to be seen in the forts of the wall and its hinterland; for example, the granaries at Birdoswald were re-modelled,[19] and the fact that the sub-floor space was in-filled suggests that the reconstructed buildings carried a different purpose from the originals. In addition, a hall-like building was built partly over a previous granary; this was supported on timber posts set on to pads. Work extended also to new sites; for example, two new fortlets are known to have guarded the road south from Carlisle – at Wreay Hall and Barrock Fell.[20] Nothing, however, is as yet known of the internal layout of these sites.

The coasts, too, received attention as they had obviously demonstrated their vulnera-

employed in Wales and at Lancaster earlier in the century. However, one feature of the re-building may have been 'learned' from the 'Saxon-shore' forts – the blocking or narrow-ing of gateways, which has been recognised at a number of northern forts, and most recently at Birdoswald on Hadrian's Wall. At that site, the north carriageway of the east gate and the south carriageway of the west gate were both closed, presumably in an effort to achieve the

Plate 71. Late Roman gold coins: Theodosius (left), from Muncaster Castle; Valentinian II (right), from Carlisle (photograph, Carlisle Archaeological Unit).

bility. As noted above, building-work belonging to the second half of the fourth century has been recognised at most coastal forts in the north-west; and there is evidence to suggest that some parts of the second-century system between Bowness-on-Solway and Maryport were brought back into use. Finds of late fourth century coins in and around Barrow-in-Furness[21] and of a gold *solidus* of Theodosius at Muncaster Castle suggest the possibility of sites in those areas too – possibly in the form of coastal towers. In addition, the east coast of northern England was given a new series of strongly built signal-towers. In all, then, Theodosius' reconstruction work in the north was a strikingly thorough attempt to take account of all of the problems encountered in the 'Barbarian Conspiracy'. It is probable that recognition of Theodosius' work is to be seen in the use of the title *Valentia* to apply to the whole of Britain, in honour of the ruling house of Valentinian.[22]

Four decades now remained before the famous 'rescript' of the emperor Honorius, informing the leaders of the Romano–British *civitates*, who had presumably sought his help against those who were in favour of pursuing more independent lines of self-defence, that there would not be further intervention from Rome to cover emergencies. This period, however, showed no obvious slackening in the north of building and maintenance activities, though it is not clear how far these were originated centrally or whether they were local initiatives, as Romano–British communities learned to become more self-reliant.

In 382 Magnus Maximus was sent to campaign in the north, though he was subsequently to achieve greater fame through his attempt to unit Gaul and Britain in a single command, and presumably to resuscitate ideas of the defunct *Imperium Galliarum*. He maintained himself until 388, and appears to have recorded some positive achievements in strengthening the security of the west coast, through the establishment of tribal protecto-

Plate 72. Birdoswald: 'sub-Roman' timber hall, built over the north granary.

Plate 73. Gauber High Pasture: Viking Long-house (photograph, Alan King). The long-house lies in a complex of structures of Romano–British origin.

rates. However, although the sources are by no means unequivocal in interpretation, it would appear that Maximus' removal of troops to Gaul once again created a volatile situation in the north; indeed it is likely that security matters in the north remained uncertain until another major outbreak, probably in 398, which brought the last positive response by Rome to British affairs. Honorius sent over the Vandal general, Stilicho, who appears to have restored order for the moment, but who either took back to Europe with him, or was closely followed by, a legion from northern Britain.[23]

94

For ten more years – the first decade of the fifth century – contact was maintained, though increasingly tenuously. It would appear that after about 402 no further supplies of money arrived to pay the army (or such as was left of it); further, evidence suggests an increasing independence within Britain. The second half of the decade saw a new series of 'local' emperors elevated by the army, which we may assume to have been the army's response to the failing support from Rome. To this may be linked the action in 408 of independently-minded Britons, perhaps influenced by the 'independent' religious views of the Pelagian heresy, in expelling Roman officials and organising the defence of Britain themselves. That this, however, was not a universal view may be assumed from the 'approach' which must have preceded Honorius' rescript. This in fact confirmed that the 'independents' had been wise: there was to be no more help from Rome, and Britain's formal place in the empire had now lapsed. These 'independent' actions, however, should not be taken to indicate a rejection of everything Roman. The rejection was political; the inhabitants of Britain after all, whether supporting or opposing Rome's current position, were *Romano–British*. As many excavations, particularly of the towns, have shown,[24] the people clearly remained for a considerable time, though perhaps in varying degrees, within the Roman cultural orbit. At Carlisle, for example, the recent discovery of a gold *solidus* of the emperor, Valentinian II (*c.* AD 392), stratified *within* a hypocaust system indicates that the building of which the hypocaust was a part must have been consciously renovated in a Roman style well into the fifth century.[25]

In general, however, the physical fate of north-western sites can only be guessed at, particularly since the means of dating in the fifth century are far from perfect: repairing of chronologically late vessels, worn late fourth-century coin-issues and finds of such vessels as African red-slip ware, all suggest a continued attempt to maintain the familiar way of life. Indeed Christianity, though not always a politically and militarily unifying force, will nonetheless have provided a link with Rome's cultural background. In the north-west, as elsewhere, we may reasonably imagine, there-fore, that Roman fortifications continued to provide protection – particularly if we judge from sites like Lancaster, Brough and Brougham, where the medieval castles were erected in some kind of association with the presumably still surviving Roman wall circuits.

The length of survival of Romano–British sites in the north-west obviously varied according to local conditions. As we have seen, some *vici* may have ceased to function relatively early; the apparent demilitarisation of the fort at Watercrook in the third century seems to have brought the life of the *vicus* to an end – even though there is some evidence for renewal of military activity in the later fourth century. At Ribchester, activity in the known *vicus* area seems to have come to an end *c.* AD 200; there is no obvious explanation of this. Some sites, such as Walton-le-Dale and Wilderspool were apparently running down during the early third century, although some activity seems to have continued into the fourth. Recent excavation at Lancaster has suggested that *vicus*-activity possibly continued until the middle of the fourth century. Clearly, no single explanation will cover all of these situations.

It may well be that in the fourth century, there was a growing tendency for military and civilian personnel alike to enjoy the protection afforded by the forts. In this regard, it is worth making the point that, in the face of troop-withdrawals during the fourth century, an increasing proportion of the garrisons were probably locally recruited: it will thus have been perfectly natural for them and their families to have regarded themselves as permanently settled in their own particular areas. Recent excavations at Birdoswald, for example, have suggested that the fort may have become more like a 'village' where a local group, perhaps with little contact with the outside world, assumed responsibility for defending and supporting itself. However, the long-term survival of such sites was unlikely; few of the north-west's fort / towns have survived as going-concerns even into the middle ages, let alone to the present day. Long-term survival required economic strength and links with the outside world. It is not surprising therefore that the north-west's survivors are generally well positioned either on navigable waterways – Chester, Wilderspool / Warrington, Walton-le-Dale / Preston, Manchester, Lancaster, Carlisle, – or at crucial places on the road-system, with the economic and military strength that that gave: hence the defended sites across Stainmore were as important in the middle ages as they had been in the Roman period. In other words, for survival, a site clearly needed to have a significance that transcended its mere place in the Roman defensive network.

In the country, the situation – due to even less excavation than in the towns – is less clear. We may assume that besides self-sufficiency two other factors must have been of crucial importance in determining the long-term survival of sites – the availability to inhabitants of markets to service and their ability to continue to work unmolested. The degree of fulfilment of these conditions must have been variable then, as well as unquantifiable now: we may, however, imagine that sites probably thrived and were left from time to time, but later returned to. A recent demonstration of this has been the discovery of Viking occupation on the site of Romano–British settlement at Gauber High Pasture in upper Ribblesdale.[26] A striking view of how long-term this process might be is the recently excavated site immediately to the south of the fort at Maiden Castle-on-Stainmore, where the latest structure on a site that showed both pre-Roman and Roman activity was a nineteenth-century cottage.

Thus, the last years of the occupation obviously show a decline in (eventually) the degree of Roman military commitment, and therefore the ability of the population to continue its established life-style. As else-where, the northern tribesmen must have been thrown increasingly on their own resources; indeed such elements of the Roman army that remained probably disbanded themselves, melting into the local community. Thus, they and the local tribesmen were now forced back into an economy where the major, perhaps sole, economic preoccupation was self-provision. Without the markets and the protection which the army had afforded, there was little else. Without the discipline which Rome had brought, the factional rivalry – no doubt largely over the ownership of resources which had characterised the pre-Roman period – returned to the north-west. The local tribesmen continued to cope with new problems but the 'Roman Interlude' was essentially over.

Footnotes – Chapter 7

1. For Hadrian's Wall, see Breeze and Dobson, 1976, 202f.
2. *RIB* 605; see Shotter and White, 1990, 60.
3. Johnson, 1980, 83ff.; Wilkes, 1965.
4. For Birdoswald, see *Britannia* XXI (1990), 316.
5. Gillam, 1949.
6. Mann, 1974.
7. Eusebius, *Life of Constantine* I.8 and 25.
8. Zosimus II.34.
9. Shotter and White, 1990, 36.
10. *RIB* 616 and 617; these statuettes are now lost (Shotter, 1973b).
11. *RIB* 601; Shotter, 1973b; Shotter and White, 1990, 59.
12. Bellhouse, 1955.
13. Simpson and Hodgson, 1947; Bellhouse, 1989, 18ff.
14. Ammianus Marcellinus XIV 5, 6–9; Hind, 1983, 1ff.

15. The term applied to it by Ammianus (XXVII.8).
16. Salway, 1981, 374f.
17. Ammianus XXVII. 3,8.
18. Potter, 1979.
19. See *Britannia* XIX (1988), 436.
20. Wreay Hall (Bellhouse, 1953); Barrock Fell (Collingwood, 1931).

21. Shotter, 1989, 43; Shotter, 1990, 239ff.
22. Johnson, 1980, 98.
23. Johnson, 1980, 103; Miller, 1975.
24. E.g. Barker, 1975.
25. See *Britannia* XX (1989), 254f.
26. King, 1978.

8. Conclusions

Over the years, a tolerably clear picture has developed of the effects of the Roman occupation of north-west England. However, there is scope for new enquiry, and although the body of knowledge has grown since the publication a decade ago of the first edition of this book, the questions which await answers remain substantially the same.

The military aspects of occupation – forts and roads – have continued to receive a good deal of attention; the fact that new forts are still located indicates that we should remain open-minded with regard to the topographical layout of the network of occupation. In particular, although some 'chinks' of light have shone, we still await a major breakthrough in the picture of occupation in southern Cumbria. A larger lacuna is the detailed chronology of occupation of military sites; very few have as yet anything more than a very basic chronological framework, and in particular we still seek to clarify by the discovery of new sites or the further treatment of evidence from existing sites the strategy and chronology of conquest. The pattern of military dispositions still requires much investigation and fresh information – in the form of writing-tablets from waterlogged deposits, and new evidence highlighted by professional and amateur fieldworkers.

Work has continued to elucidate chronological and topographical factors concerning the occupation of the coastline of north-west England, although we still require more information on the flexibility of treatment, and in particular, how much use may have been made of the sites in the more troubled times of the fourth century.

The *vici*, too, leave many unanswered questions; in particular we have no satisfactory explanation as to why a considerable number of them seem not to have outlasted the mid-third century. Were there local conditions which were responsible, or was a more general factor at play? As yet we do not have, except on aerial photographs, anything like the full plan of a *vicus* in the north-west. This not only denies us a full picture of all the buildings that these small towns might support, but also a reasonable idea of the make-up of the population. The organisation of the *vici* also requires further research.

In the countryside, the need is for excavation to answer some of the basic problems about development, chronology and economy; besides this, the question of the economic relationship between the farms and the Roman sites needs further exploration; so too does the way in which land was allocated, and the nature of the relationship between the ex-soldiers given land at the time of their discharge and the native farmers who were the descendants of those whom the army had originally conquered. In this connection it should be remembered that large areas of the north-west have not been subjected to detailed field-work and have not as yet been covered by aerial reconnaissance.

This indicates where progress has been made and a few of the problems still requiring attention. In outline we have a fair picture of the development of the north-west in the period of Roman occupation. Studies of the immediately post-Roman period and of the so-called 'Dark Ages' may well help to illuminate the question of whether Roman influence went deep or whether it was a passing phase, though it has to be admitted that Christianity in the celtic west must have done a good deal to preserve a Roman tradition.

In conclusion, however, we now know enough to lay aside the older notions of an iron-fisted conqueror controlling a people generally hostile or sullenly passive. Rather, *Dea Brigantia* presided over territory that was in its way as Romanised as many other parts of the empire.

Appendix I

The Brigantes, Venutius and Cartimandua

The two fullest accounts of the Brigantes to have survived in classical writers are those of the historian, Cornelius Tacitus, in *Histories* III.45 and *Annals* XII.40. Some of the problems inherent in the passages have been discussed in the main body of the text (see above in Chapter 3).

The passage from the *Annals*, although written later (*c.* AD 115), describes the earlier of the two situations – that is, in the 50s and 60s. The passage from the *Histories* (written *c.* AD 102) covers events leading up to Roman intervention in the 70s. Whilst there are shades of difference between the two accounts, both stress that at least some of the squabbling between Venutius and Cartimandua remained internal to the Brigantes, although the former was able to call on help from outside – perhaps from north Wales. It is also tolerably clear that the overall effect of the tensions was actually to maintain the *status quo*. The fact that Tacitus compares Venutius and Caratacus as warriors is itself of interest, and would certainly help to explain how the Brigantes were so formidable under him (that is, during Cerialis' governorship), and so much easier when he had been removed (that is, when Agricola went through the area in a single season).

I: Annals XII. 40

'Following the Roman capture of Caratacus, the foremost military thinker left in Britain was Venutius who, as I have already recorded,[*] was a Brigantian. Whilst he was married to queen Cartimandua, he enjoyed Roman protection and was a loyal ally; however, after they split up he attacked her and even became embroiled in hostilities against us. At first the Brigantian leaders confined themselves to fighting each other, as Cartimandua cleverly trapped Venutius' brother and dependents. Before long, however, Cartimandua's enemies became angry at the disgrace which they perceived to be involved in being ruled by a woman, and they attacked her kingdom with a hand-picked band of strong, young, warriors. We were ready for this, and made a pre-emptive strike with a force of auxiliaries which we sent in to support Cartimandua. Although these support-troops achieved little to start with, they were eventually successful; a similar reward attended the efforts of the legion which was commanded by Caesius Nasica. Didius Gallus (i.e. the provincial governor), an elderly man who was by now resting on his laurels, was happy to keep the enemy at arm's length through the actions of his subordinates.'

---

[*]   This is a reference evidently to an earlier mention of Venutius in a portion of the *Annals* which is now lost (presumably in books VII-X, which dealt with the reign of Gaius Caligula and Claudius' early years).

'The persistent rumours of civil war encouraged British morale and Venutius capitalised upon this. He was a man with a naturally violent disposition who hated everything to do with Rome. At this time, his temper was made worse as a result of a bitter personal feud with queen Cartimandua. Her influence lay in the nobility of her birth, and she had ruled over the Brigantes for some time; her power had increased as the result of her treacherous capture of king Caratacus which, it was generally thought, was the crowning glory of the emperor Claudius' British triumph. So she became wealthy, and enjoyed the luxurious lifestyle associated with success. She tired of her husband, Venutius, and gave herself instead to Vellocatus, her husband's armour-bearer, and shared her kingdom with him. The immediate effect of this was a shock-wave which ran throughout the royal family.

'The Brigantian tribesmen retained their loyalty to Venutius, although the new husband prospered as a result of the queen's infatuation with him and the harsh control which she exercised over her people. So Venutius called up help from outside, and this prompted the Brigantes to defect from Cartimandua who was left in real danger of defeat. So she appealed for Roman assistance; in the event, our auxiliary cavalry and infantry units, after an uphill struggle, rescued the queen from her immediate peril. As a result, Venutius was left in control of the kingdom, whilst we had a full-scale war on our hands.'

The problems of relating these passages are considerable, largely because of the vagueness of Tacitus' chronology; the only events which can be dated are the capture of Caratacus (AD 51) and the Roman civil war (AD 68–9). For discussions, see Hanson and Campbell, 1986 and Braund, 1984.

Similarly vague in chronology and topography is Tacitus' account of Agricola's second campaign in which he appears *formally* to have added the Brigantes to the province.

Life of Agricola, 20

'In early summer, Agricola prepared his army for the year's campaigning season. He was himself much in evidence on the march, praising those who were well-disciplined and chivvying the stragglers. Agricola chose the camp-sites himself and personally reconnoitred estuaries and woods. In all of this, the enemy was given little respite from the sudden raids which the Romans launched on them. When he had made sufficient use of such intimidatory tactics, he would take the heat off and show them the attraction of peace. As a result, many groups, which had up to that time lived independently, gave hostages, laid aside their hostility and accepted being fenced in with forts and garrisons. This was all done with such attention to detail that no new area had ever become part of the province with as little trouble as this.'

Appendix II

Known Dispositions of Roman Units in North-West England

Chester	Leg II Adiutrix
	Leg XX Valeria Victrix (inscriptions give dates from mid-second to mid-third century)
Manchester	Vex of Leg II and III Italica (late second century)
	Coh I Frisiavonum
	Coh III Bracaraugustanorum (possibly second century)
Castleshaw	Coh III Bracaraugustanorum
Ribchester	Ala II Asturum
	Numerus Equitum (later Ala) Sarmatarum (third century)
Lancaster	Ala Augusta
	Ala Sebosiana (mid-third century)
	Numerus Barcariorum
Bainbridge	Coh VI Nerviorum (early third century)
Bowes	Coh IIII Breucorum (130s)
	Coh I Thracum (late second to mid-third century)
Kirkby Thore	Ala
	Numerus militum Syrorum Sagittariorum
	Coh? Gallorum
	Coh I Vangionum (?)
	Cuneus Frisionum Germanorum
	Numerus Equitum Stratonicianorum
Hardknott	Coh IIII Delmatorum (Hadrianic)
Moresby	Coh II Thracum
	Coh II Lingonum
Maryport	Coh I Hispanorum Equitata (Hadrianic)
	Coh I Delmatarum (Antonine)
	Coh I Baetasiorum
Beckfoot	Coh II Pannoniorum
Papcastle	Cuneus Frisionum Aballavensium (mid-third century)
Old Carlisle	Ala Augusta (late second to mid-third century)
Old Penrith	Coh II Gallorum Equitata (mid-third century)
	Vex Marsacarum (mid-third century)
	Vex Germanorum (mid-third century)
Stanwix	Ala Augusta Petriana milliaria torquata (late second century)
Carlisle	All British legions are recorded (II Augusta, VI Victrix, IX Hispana, XX Valeria Victrix)
Netherby	Coh I Nervana
	Coh I Aelia Hispanorum milliaria equitata (early to mid-third century)
Bewcastle	Coh I Dacorum
Vindolanda	Coh II Nerviorum (?)
	Coh III Nerviorum
	Coh IIII Gallorum (third century)

Great Chesters	Vex Raetorum Gaesatorum
	Coh Raetorum (mid-second century)
	Coh VI Nerviorum
	Coh II Asturum (early to mid-third century)
Carvoran	Coh I Hamiorum Sagittariorum (Hadrianic, late Antonine)
	Coh II Delmatarum
	Coh I Batavorum
	Numerus
Birdoswald	Coh I Aelia Dacorum (third century)
	Coh I Thracum C. R. (early third century)
	Coh ? (late third century)
Castlesteads	Coh IIII Gallorum Equitata
	Coh II Tungrorum milliaria equitata C. L. (mid-third century)
Burgh-by-Sands	Coh I Nervana Germanorum milliaria equitata
	Numerus Maurorum Aurelianorum (mid-third century)
Bowness-on-Solway	Coh? (mid-third century)
Birrens	Coh II Tungrorum milliaria equitata C. L. (Antonine)
	Coh I Nervana Germanorum milliaria equitata
Melandra Castle	Coh I Frisiavonum
Brough-on-Noe	Coh I Aquitanorum
Whitley Castle	Coh II Nerviorum

Appendix III

Dated Building-Inscriptions from Forts in North-West England

A. Vespasian	Chester (AD 79)	*RIB* 463 & *EE* IX, 1039; *Britannia* I (1970), 292f.
B. Trajan	Chester (AD 102–17)	*RIB* 464
	Lancaster (AD 102–17)	*RIB* 604
	Melandra (AD 98–117)	*RIB* 208
C. Hadrian	Bowes (AD 130–3)	*RIB* 739
	Hardknott	*JRS* LV (1965), 222
	Moresby (AD 128–38)	*RIB* 801
	Maryport (AD 117–38)	*RIB* 851
	Netherby	*RIB* 974
	Bewcastle	*RIB* 995
	Great Chesters (AD 128–38)	*RIB* 1736
D. Antoninus Pius	Castlesteads (AD 140–4)	*RIB* 1997
	Birrens (AD 157–8)	*RIB* 2110
	Brough-on-Noe (AD 158)	*RIB* 283
E. Marcus Aurelius	Ribchester (AD 163–6)	*RIB* 589
	Hardknott (AD 163–6)	*RIB* 793
	Vindolanda (AD 163–6)	*RIB* 1703
	Great Chesters (AD 163–6)	*RIB* 1737
	Carvoran (AD 163–6)	*RIB* 1809
F. Septimius Severus	Chester (AD 194–6)	*RIB* 465
	Manchester	*RIB* 581
	Bainbridge (AD 205–8)	*RIB* 722, 723
	Greta Bridge (AD 205–8)	*RIB* 746
	Bowes (AD 205–8)	*RIB* 740
	Brough (AD 197)	*RIB* 757
	Birdoswald (AD 198–209)	*RIB* 1910
G. Caracalla	Maryport (AD 211–17)	*RIB* 832, 850
	Old Carlisle (AD 213)	*RIB* 928
	Netherby (AD 213)	*RIB* 976, 977
	Vindolanda (AD 213)	*RIB* 1705
	Birdoswald (AD 211–17)	*RIB* 1911
	Whitley Castle (AD 213 and 215–16)	*RIB* 1202, 1203
	Lancaster (?)	*Britannia* XVII (1986), 436
H. Elagabalus	Birdoswald (AD 219)	*RIB* 1914
I. Severus Alexander	Ribchester (AD 222–35)	*RIB* 587
	Old Penrith (AD 222–35)	*RIB* 919, 929
	Old Carlisle (AD 222–35)	*RIB* 929
	Netherby (AD 222)	*RIB* 978
	Vindolanda (AD 223)	*RIB* 1706
	Great Chesters (AD 225)	*RIB* 1738
J. Gordian III	Maryport (AD 238–44)	*RIB* 854
	Stanwix (AD 238–44)	*RIB* 2027
K. Postumus	Lancaster (AD 262–6)	*RIB* 605
L. Diocletian	Birdoswald (AD 297–305)	*RIB* 1912

Appendix IV

Names of Roman Sites in North-West England

The names by which Roman sites were known have proved extraordinarily elusive; relating known names to particular sites is hazardous, and confidence in such an exercise is not enhanced by the fact that new major sites continue to appear – for example, in recent years, Burgh I and Blennerhasset – and speculation remains concerning the possible existence of other sites as yet unknown.

The most reliable evidence is that which derives from inscriptions found at the sites in question; in this way we can be virtually certain of four identifications – Ribchester / Bremetennacum, Chesterholm / Vindolanda, Birdoswald / Banna and Chester / Deva. It further seems likely that on epigraphic grounds we can accept that Old Carlisle (Red Dial) was either Maglone or Magis, whilst writing tablets found at Vindolanda and Carlisle leave little doubt that Carlisle was Luguvalium. It has also been shown (by Hassall, 1976) that the sequence of forts at the western end of Hadrian's Wall can be at least partially reconstructed thus –

Bowness-on-Solway	Maia
Burgh-by-Sands	Aballava
Stanwix	Uxellodunum (though probably also called Petriana)
Castlesteads	Camboglanna
Birdoswald	Banna

The bulk of other known names of Roman sites appear in three extant or partially extant documents – the *Antonine Itinerary*, the *Notitia Dignitatum* and the *Ravenna Cosmography*. These present us with sequences or collections of names, which require interpretation before we can propose identifications for them; even then we have to admit that we have too small a number of 'certainties' to be able to offer reliable identifications in any but a few cases.

The Antonine Itinerary

This document, compiled in the early third century AD, consists of lists of names, separated by distances and arranged in 'routes'. Roman sites in north-west England are found in Routes II, V and X. It should be noted that a fundamental problem attaches to interpretation: since the document was compiled early in the third century AD, we should assume that sites which are named were occupied at the time of compilation. As we have seen, clear chronologies have as yet been established for only a few sites, leaving us in doubt in some cases whether they were in fact occupied at the relevant time.

Route X ran for 150 miles from Clanoventa to Mediolanum, traditionally Ravenglass to Whitchurch (in Shropshire). Intermediate points on the route are Galava, Alone, Galacum, Bremetonnacum, Coccium, Mamucium and Condate; of the nine sites, only Bremetonnacum can on epigraphic grounds be identified – that is, with Ribchester. There is no pressing reason to place the beginning of the route at Ravenglass; indeed there is a strong possibility in view of the dedication from Lancaster to the god, Ialonus, (possibly a river-deity) that Galava, Alone and Galacum should be taken as the names of sites on the river Lune – respectively Low Borrow Bridge (Galava), Burrow-in-Lonsdale (Alone) and Lancaster (Galacum). Clanoventa might then be suitably identified with Ambleside; the disposition and role of the fort (described in chapter 4) are well encapsulated in a name which means 'market by the clear water'. South of Ribchester, the route makes for Manchester (Mamucium) and Northwich (Condate), passing through Coccium; in view of recent work at Wigan, there is no difficulty in associating it with Coccium, although there is a view that Coccium might be a site as yet unknown – possibly in the Bolton area.

Route II ran for 481 miles from the northern frontier to the port of Richborough in Kent; it specifies initial stages from Blatobulgium and Castra Exploratorum to Luguvallum. Luguvallum (or Luguvalium) is to be identified with Carlisle, and the preceding sites of Netherby (Castra Exploratorum / Fort of the Scouts) and Birrens (Blatobulgium) seem well-founded. South of Carlisle, the route runs to Voreda, Brovonacae, Verterae, Lavatrae and then through Cataractone and Isurium to Eburacum. There is little doubt that the last three are Catterick, Aldborough and York, and that therefore the route crosses from west to east over Stainmore. The stated distances are consistent with stages from Carlisle to Old Penrith (Voreda), Kirkby Thore (Brovonacae), Brough (Verterae) and Bowes (Lavatrae).

Route V ran for 442 miles from London to Carlisle (Luguvalium); the latter portion of this route proceeds through York (Eburacum) and Aldborough (Isubrigantum) to Catterick (Cataractone), and thence to Bowes (Lavatrae) and Brough (Verterae). Thus far this route is identical to Route II – but in reverse. In Route V, however, there is no mention of Brovonacae (Kirkby Thore) or Voreda (Old Penrith); instead, Brocavum lies between Brough and Carlisle. The most suitable location for Brocavum is Brougham which, like its medieval counterpart, stood at the important junction of the Stainmore and the north / south routes.

From the *Antonine Itinerary*, therefore, sixteen sites in north-west England can be associated with names with varying degrees of certainty.

The Notitia Dignitatum

Most of the problems raised by this document are too far-reaching for discussion in the present context; dating and purpose have been the subjects of much speculation, as have the identities of site-names and military units listed as belonging to the command of the officer known as the *Dux Britanniarum* (Duke of the Britains), who was based at York and controlled the northern frontier-area. It is generally held that most of the information belongs to the second half of the fourth century, although that concerning the 'wall sub-section' *may* date from the previous century. At the same time, great problems are caused by the fact that, with the exception of the 'wall sub-section', the sites are not apparently listed in conformity with any geographical or military logic; further, there is some evidence of textual disturbance in the portion dealing with the western end of Hadrian's Wall.

The 'wall sub-section' contains some names familiar from the Rudge Cup, although there are problems of textual interpretation. It is reasonable to suppose that the western sequence includes Castlesteads (Amboglanna) and Stanwix (Uxellodunum / Petrianae); however, the name (though not the military unit) of Birdoswald has been lost. Burgh-by-Sands appears as Aballaba, although there is no apparent listing of Drumburgh or Bowness-on-Solway. Beyond Aballaba, the names Congavata, Axelodunum, Gabrosentum, Tunnocelum and Glannibanta have been taken to be the forts of the Cumberland coast – Beckfoot, Maryport, Burrow Walls, Moresby and Ravenglass; of the military units mentioned in the *Notitia*-list some are known from epigraphic evidence to have been garrisoned at coastal sites. For example, Cohors I Hispanorum is known at Maryport, whilst Cohors II Lingonum and Cohors II Thracum are both evidenced at Moresby. Further, a lead sealing of Cohors I Aelia Classica was found in the 1977 / 78 excavations at Ravenglass.

It is possible in view of this that we could postulate identifications of Beckfoot / Congavata, Maryport / Axelodunum, Moresby / Gabrosentum and Ravenglass / Tunnocelum. Glannibanta could then be identified with Ambleside (Clanoventa of the *Antonine Itinerary*). There is then no reason why Alione should not be Burrow-in-Lonsdale, particularly since the next site listed is Bremetenracum / Ribchester.

The Duke's list in the *Notitia* also includes Lavatrae, Verterae, and Braboniacum; these appear to preserve the sequence over Stainmore marked in the *Antonine Itinerary* of Bowes, Brough and Kirkby Thore. Moreover, the unit placed at Brough, the *numerus directorum* (or Unit of Dispatchers) would be appropriate for a site which has produced such a large and variable collection of lead sealings for official packages. Maglone and Magis are placed after Braboniacum and, as we have seen, there is some reason to suppose that one of these might be Old Carlisle.

This leaves unidentified Magis or Maglone, Longovicium (which appears at this point but which *may* be a north-eastern site), Derventio (often taken as Papcastle, which in view of its probable significance would be expected to have had a place in the list), and finally Olenacum and Virosidum (which could be Ilkley and Bainbridge). These postulated identifications do not restore total logic to the sequence in the *Notitia*, or solve all of the problems, but they do provide some geographical connections and sequences.

The Ravenna Cosmography

This document of the seventh century appears to derive in part from a road-map; lists of names radiate from centres which are mentioned once and subsequently have to be understood at the commencement of each route for which they are the starting-point. Thus Manchester (Mautio) is the starting-point for four routes – to Alicuna (Ilkley), to Camulodunum (Slack?), and to Caluvio (Lancaster), whilst the fourth runs to Bresnetenacum Veteranorum (Ribchester) into west Yorkshire. Place-names are not necessarily listed on *every* route on which they feature. Thus Ribchester is not listed on the route leading from Manchester to Lancaster, but simply on that which heads into west Yorkshire.

Within the list that leads from Manchester, there appear to be subsidiary 'departure-points'; thus after Caluvio (Lancaster) came Galluvio (Low Borrow Bridge), Medibogdo, Cantiventi, Iuliocenon and Gabrocentio. Of these Medibogdo ('fort in the middle of a bow') would seem to be a strong description of Watercrook, and thus represents a fresh departure from Lancaster. It would appear to lead to Ambleside (Cantiventi, possibly, though not necessarily, to be identified with Clanoventa), and then to Iuliocenon (Tunnocelum, and probably Ravenglass) and Gabrocentio (Gabrosentum / Moresby). Alauna, which follows Gabrocentio, has usually been identified with Maryport, but might in fact represent a further departure from Lancaster along the Lune Valley, to Burrow-in-Lonsdale (Alauna). It has to be said that this leaves Bribra, Maio, Olerica, Derventio and Ravonia hard to identify, although Bribra might be Virosidum (Bainbridge), from which two routes lead – one into Yorkshire (To Malton / Derventio), the other to Kirkby Thore (probably to be identified with Ravonia).

Kirkby Thore then becomes a new departure-point: first, a route leads to Valteris (Brough), and then a second to Old Penrith (Bereda) and Carlisle (Lagubalium). A third then proceeds northwards to a new centre – Magnis (or Carvoran); from here one road leads to Gabaglanda (Castlesteads), another to Vindolanda. A subsequent starting-point is Banna (Birdoswald) leading first to Uxellodunum (possibly, as we have seen, an alternative name for Stanwix), Avalava (Burgh-by-Sands) and Maia (Bowness-on-Solway); a second route from Birdoswald leads to Fanum Cocidi, which was probably Bewcastle.

Further south, the *Cosmography*-listing provides a clear sequence of Deva Victrix (Chester) and Condate (Northwich).

Although much remains unclear, this short discussion indicates that there is room for re-arrangement and re-thinking of traditional identifications, although fresh certainty can be applied only with the discovery of new inscriptions which can provide us with new firm identifications.

A word should finally be said about the site Portus Setantiorum which figures in the *Geography* of Ptolemy of Alexandria. It is usually assumed that this represents a site that has been lost through coastal change and now lies off Fleetwood beneath the waters of the Lune Estuary.

It is a story that readily lends itself to romantic embroidery. We should, however, bear in mind that the Setantii *may* have lived in southern Cumbria, and the Portus Setantiorum may be an elusive site near the southern end of Lake Windermere.

For further reading on the place-name evidence, see particularly –

Rivet, 1970 – *The Antonine Itinerary*
Goodburn and Bartholomew, 1976 – *The Notitia Dignitatum*
Richmond and Crawford, 1949 – *The Ravenna Cosmography*

Summary of evidence for
Roman site-names in North West-England

Site	Epigraphic	It. Ant.	Not. Dign.	Rav. Cosm.	Other
Ambleside		CLANOVENTA	GLANNIBANTA	CANTIVENTI	
Beckfoot			CONGAVATA		
Bewcastle				FANUM COCIDI	
Birdoswald	BANNA			BANNA	BANNA
Birrens		BLATOBULGIUM			
Blennerhasset					
Bowes		LAVATRAE	LAVATRES	LAVARIS	
Bowness				MAIA	MAIA
Brough		VERTERAE	VERTERAE	VALTERIS	
Brougham		BROCAVUM			
Burgh-by-Sands			ABALLABA	AVALAVA	ABALLABA
Burrow-in-Lonsdale		ALONE	ALIONE	ALAUNA	
Burrow Walls					
Caermote					
Carlisle	LUGUVALIUM	LUGUVALLUM		LAGUBALIUM	
Castleshaw					
Castlesteads			AMBOGLANNA	GABAGLANDA	CAMBOGLANS
Chester	DEVA			DEVA VICTRIX	
Drumburgh					
Hardknott					
Kirkbride					
Kirkby Thore		BROVONACAE	BRABONIACUM	RAVONIA	
Kirkham					
Lancaster		GALACUM		CALUVIO	
Low Borrow Bridge		GALAVA			
Manchester		MAMUCIUM			MAUTIO
Maryport				AXELODUNUM	
Moresby			GABROSENTUM	GABROCENTIO	
Netherby		CASTRA EXPLORATORUM			
Northwich		CONDATE		CONDATE	
Old Carlisle	MAGIS (?)		MAGIS (?)		
Old Penrith		VOREDA		BEREDA	
Papcastle			DERVENTIO (?)		
Ravenglass			TUNNOCELUM	IULIOCENON	
Ribchester	BREMETENNACUM	BREMETONNACUM	BREMETENRACUM	BRESNETENACUM VETERANORUM	
Stanwix			PETRIANAE		UXELODUM
Walton-le-Dale					
Watercrook				MEDIBOGDO	
Wigan		COCCIUM			
Wilderspool					

Notes

Note: The majority of the military sites discussed in this book have seen excavation over a long period of time, which has meant that all but a few items from the detailed references for individual sites has had, for reasons of space, to be omitted. However, extremely useful summaries and bibliographies for the military sites may be found in M. J. Jones, *Roman Fort-Defences to AD 117*, British Archaeological Reports No. 21 (Oxford 1975). In addition, the annual surveys entitled 'Roman Britain in 19. . .', contained first in *Journal of Roman Studies* and (since 1970) in *Britannia* provide on-going and up-to-the-minute summaries of current excavations. At the time of writing, several excavation reports and site studies are awaited or actually in the press. Carlisle, The Lanes (M. R. McCarthy), Walton-le-Dale, Papcastle and Ribchester (A. C. H. Olivier), Birdoswald (A. Wilmot).

Abbreviations

Arch. Ael.	*Archaeologia Aeliana*
Arch. Journ.	*Archaeological Journal*
BAR	*British Archaeological Reports*
CAJ	*Journal of the Chester Archaeological Society*
CW²	*Transactions of the Cumberland and Westmorland Antiquarian and Archaeological Society*
EE	*Ephemeris Epigraphica*
GMAJ	*Greater Manchester Archaeological Journal*
JRS	*Journal of Roman Studies*
PSAS	*Proceedings of the Society of Antiquaries of Scotland*
RCHM	*Royal Commission on Historical Monuments, England: Westmorland (London 1936)*
RIB	*Roman Inscriptions of Britain*
Scot. Arch. Forum	*Scottish Archaeological Forum*
SHA	*Scriptores Historiae Augustae*
YAJ	*Yorkshire Archaeological Journal*

Bibliography

Austen, P. S. (1990). *Bewcastle and Old Penrith*. Kendal

Barker, P. (1975). Excavations at the Baths Basilica at Wroxeter 1966–74. *Britannia* VI, 106–17.

Bellhouse, R. L. (1953). A Roman Fort at Wreay Hall, near Carlisle, *CW2* 53, 49–51.

Bellhouse, R. L. (1954a). A newly discovered Roman Fort at Park House, near Carlisle. *CW2* 54, 9–16.

Bellhouse, R. L. (1954b). Roman Sites on the Cumberland Coast 1954. *CW2*, 54, 28–55.

Bellhouse, R. L. (1955). The Roman Fort at Burrow Walls, near Workington. *CW2* 55, 30–45.

Bellhouse, R. L. (1960a). The Roman Forts near Caermote. *CW2* 60, 20–3.

Bellhouse, R. L. (1960b). Excavations in Eskdale, the Muncaster Roman Kilns. *CW2* 60, 1–12.

Bellhouse, R. L. (1967). The Aughertree Fell Enclosures. *CW2* 67, 26–30.

Bellhouse, R. L. (1971). Roman Tileries at Scalesceugh and Brampton. *CW2* 71, 35–44.

Bellhouse, R. L. (1981). Hadrian's Wall: The Limiting Ditches in the Cardurnock Peninsular. *Britannia* XII, 135–42.

Bellhouse, R. L. (1989). *Roman Sites on the Cumberland Coast*. Kendal.

Bellhouse, R. L. and Richardson, G. G. S. (1982). The Trajanic Fort at Kirkbride; the terminus of the Stanegate Frontier. *CW2* 82, 35–50.

Birley, A. R. (1973). Petillius Cerialis and the Conquest of Brigantia. *Britannia* IV, 179–90.

Birley, A. R. (1975). Agricola, the Flavian Dynasty and Tacitus, in Levick, B. (ed.) *The Ancient Historian and his Materials*, pp. 139–54. Farnborough, Hants.

Birley, E. B. (1932). Materials for the History of Roman Brougham. *CW2* 32, 124–39.

Birley, E. B. (1946). The Roman Site at Burrow-in-Lonsdale. *CW2* 46, 126–56.

Birley, E. B. (1947). The Roman Fort at Low Borrow Bridge. *CW2* 47, 1–19.

Birley, E. B. (1951). The Roman Fort and Settlement at Old Carlisle. *CW2* 51, 16–39.

Birley, E. B. (1953). The Roman Milestone at Middleton-in-Lonsdale. *CW2* 53, 52–62.

Birley, E. B. (1958). The Roman Fort at Brough-under-Stainmore. *CW2* 58, 31–56.

Birley, E. B. (1963). Roman Papcastle. *CW2* 63, 96–125.

Birley, R. N. (1977). *Vindolanda; A Roman Frontier Post on Hadrian's Wall*. London.

Blake, B. (1959). Excavations of Native (Iron Age) Sites in Cumberland 1956–8. *CW2* 59, 1–14.

Bowman, A. K. and Thomas, J. D. (1983). *Vindolanda: The Latin Writing Tablets*. Britannia Monographs 4. London.

Branigan, K. (1980). Villas in the North: Change in the Rural Landscape, in Branigan, K. (ed.) *Rome and the Brigantes*, pp. 18–27. Sheffield.

Braund, D. (1984). Some Observations on Cartimandua, *Britannia* XV. 1–6.

Breeze, D. J. (1975). The Abandonment of the Antonine Wall: its date and Implications. *Scot. Arch. Forum* VII, 67–78

Breeze, D. J. (1988). The Roman Army in Cumbria. *CW2* 88, 9–22.

Breeze, D. J. and Dobson, B. (1976). *Hadrian's Wall*. London.

Bruton, F. A. (1908). *Excavation of the Roman Forts at Castleshaw*. Manchester.

Bruton, F. A. (1909). *The Roman Fort at Manchester*. Manchester.

Charlesworth, D. (1964). Recent Work at Kirkby Thore. *CW2* 64, 61–75.

Charlesworth, D. (1965). Excavations at Papcastle 1961–2. *CW2* 65, 102–14.

Clare, T. (1989). The Prehistoric Landscape, pp. 9–27 in Rollinson, W. (ed.) *The Lake District: Landscape Heritage*. Newton Abbot.

Collingwood, R. G. (1931). A Roman Fortlet on Barrock Fell, near Low Hesket. *CW2* 31, 111–18.

Collingwood, W. G. (1908–9). Report on an Exploration of the Romano–British Settlement at Ewe Close. *CW2* 9, 295–309.

Davies, R. W. (1977). Cohors I Hispanorum and the Garrisons of Maryport. *CW2* 77, 7–16.

Davies, R. W. (1971). The Roman Military Diet. *Britannia* II, 122–42.

Edwards, B. J. N. (1971). Roman Finds from Contrebis, *CW²* 71, 17–34.

Edwards, B. J. N. (1972). *Ribchester*. National Trust Handbook.

Edwards, B. J. N. and Webster, P. V. (1985–8). *Ribchester Excavations*. Cardiff.

Evans, J. and Scull, C. (1990). Fieldwork on the Roman fort site at Blennerhasset, Cumbria. *CW²* 90, 127–38.

Gibbons, P. (1989). Excavations and Observations at Kirkby Thore. *CW²* 89, 93–130.

Gillam, J. P. (1949). Also, Along the Line of the Wall. *CW²* 49, 38–58.

Goodburn, R. and Bartholomew, P. (eds.), (1976). Aspects of the Notitia Dignitatum. *British Archaeological Reports* 15. Oxford.

Graystone, P. (1992). *Walking Roman Roads in Bowland*. Lancaster.

Hanson, W. S., with Daniels, C. M., Dore J. N., and Gillam, J. P. (1979). The Agricolan Supply-base at Red House, Corbridge. *Arch. Ael.* ⁵ VII, 1–88.

Hanson, W. S. (1987). *Agricola and the Conquest of the North*. London.

Hanson, W. S. and Campbell, D. B. (1986). The Brigantes: From Clientage to Conquest. *Britannia* XVII, 73–89.

Hanson, W. S. and Maxwell, G. (1983). *The Antonine Wall: Rome's North-West Frontier*. Edinburgh.

Hartley, B. R. (1966). Some Problems of the Roman Military Occupation of Northern England. *Northern History* I, 7–10.

Hartley, B. R. (1972). The Roman Occupations of Scotland: the Evidence of Samian Ware. *Britannia* III, 1–55.

Hartley, B. R. (1980). The Brigantes and the Roman Army, in Branigan K. (ed.) *Rome and the Brigantes*, pp. 2–7. Sheffield.

Hassall, M. W. C. (1976). Britain in the Notitia. In Goodburn R. and Bartholomew P. (eds.): *vide supra* pp. 103–17.

Henig, M. (1984). *Religion in Roman Britain*. London.

Heurgon, J. (1951). The Amiens Patera. *JRS* 41, 22–4.

Higham, N. J. (1978). Early Field Survival in North Cumbria, in Bowen, H. C. and Fowler, P. J. (eds.) *Early Land Allotment in the British Isles*. British Archaeological Reports 48, pp. 119–25. Oxford.

Higham, N. J. (1979). An Aerial Survey of the Upper Lune Valley, in Higham N. J. (ed.) *The Changing Past*, pp. 31–8. Manchester.

Higham, N. J. (1980). Native Settlements West of the Pennines, in Branigan, K. (ed.) *Rome and the Brigantes*, pp. 41–7. Sheffield.

Higham, N. J. (1982). 'Native' Settlements on the North Slopes of the Lake District. *CW²* 82, 29–33.

Higham, N. J. (1986). *The Northern Counties to AD 1000*, London

Higham, N. J. and Jones, G. D. B. (1975). Frontier, Forts and Farmers. *Arch. Journ.* 132, 16–53.

Hildyard, E. J. W. (1951). Renewed Excavation at Low Borrow Bridge. *CW²* 51, 40–66.

Hildyard, E. J. W. (1954). Excavations at Burrow-in-Lonsdale. *CW²* 54, 66–101.

Hill, P. V. (1970). *The Undated Coins of Rome, AD 98–148*. London.

Hinchcliffe, J. and Williams, J. H. (1992) *Roman Warrington*. Manchester.

Hind, J. G. F. (1977). The 'Genounian' Part of Britain. *Britannia* VIII, 229–34.

Hind, J. G. F. (1983). Who betrayed Britain to the Barbarians in AD 367? *Northern History* 19, 1–7.

Hogg, R. (1965). Excavation of the Roman Auxiliary tilery, Brampton. *CW²* 65, 133–68.

Jarrett, M. G. (1976). *Maryport, Cumbria: A Roman Fort and its Garrison*. Kendal.

Johnson, A. S. (1980). *Later Roman Britain*. (London)

Jones, G. C. and Price, J. (1985). Excavations at the Wiend, Wigan, 1982–4. *GMAJ* 1, 25–33.

Jones, G. D. B. (1968). The Romans in the North West. *Northern History* III, 1–26.

Jones, G. D. B. (1970). Roman Lancashire. *Arch. Journ.* 127, 237–45.

Jones, G. D. B. (1972). Excavations at Northwich (Condate). *Arch. Journ.* 128, 31–77.

Jones, G. D. B. (1974). *Roman Manchester*. Altrincham.

Jones, G. D. B. (1975). The North-Western Interface, in Fowler, P. J. (ed.) *Recent work in Rural Archaeology*, pp. 93–106. Bradford-on-Avon.

Jones, G. D. B. (1979). The Future of Aerial Photography in the North, in Higham, N. J. (ed.) *The Changing Past*, 75–87. Manchester.

Jones, G. D. B. (1980). Archaeology and Coastal Change in the North-West, in Thompson, F. H. (ed.) *Archaeology and Coastal Change*, pp. 87–102. London.

Jones, G. D. B. (1982). The Solway Frontier: Interim Report 1976–81. *Britannia* XIII, 284–97.

Jones, G. D. B. and Higham, N. J. (1985). *The Carvetii*. London.

Jones, G. D. B. and Shotter, D. C. A. (1988). *Roman Lancaster*. Manchester.

Jones, G. D. B. and Wild, J. P. (1970). Manchester University Excavations at Brough-on-Noe (Navio) 1969. *Derbys. Arch. Journ.* 70, 99–106.

Jones, M. J. (1975). Roman Fort-Defences to AD 117. *British Archaeological Reports* 21. Oxford.

Jones, M. J. (1977). Archaeological Work at Brough-under-Stainmore 1971–2, I. the Roman Discoveries. *CW²* 77, 35–50.

Jones, R. F. J. (1981). Change in the Frontier, Northern Britain in the Third Century, in King A. and Henig, M. *The Roman West in the Third Century*, BAR(S) 109, pp. 393–414.

Keppie, L. J. F. and Walker, J. J. (1981). Fortlets on the Antonine Wall at Seabegs Wood, Kinneil and Cleddans. *Britannia* XII, 143–62.

King. A. (1978). Gauber High Pasture, Ribblehead – an interim report, in Hall, R. A. (ed.) *Viking Age York and the North*, CBA Research Report 27, pp. 21–5. London.

Lowndes, R. A. C. (1963). 'Celtic' fields, farms and burial mounds in the Lune Valley. *CW²* 63, 77–95.

Lowndes, R. A. C. (1964). Excavation of a Romano–British Farmstead at Eller Beck. *CW²* 64, 1–13.

Mann, J. C. (1974). The Northern Frontier after AD 369, Glasgow *Arch. Journ.* 3, 34–42.

Manning, W. H. (1975). Economic influences on land use in the military areas of the Highland Zone during the Roman period, in Evans, J. G., Limbrey, S. and Cleere, H. (eds.) *The Effect of Man on the Landscape: the Highland Zone*. CBA Research Report 11, pp. 112–16. London.

Maxwell, G. (1990). *A Battle Lost*. Edinburgh.

McCarthy, M. R. (1980). *Carlisle, A Frontier City*. Carlisle.

McCarthy, M. R. (1990). *A Roman, Anglian and Medieval Site at Blackfriars Street*. Kendal.

McCarthy, M. R. (1991). *Roman Waterlogged Remains at Castle Street*. Kendal.

Miller, M. (1975). Stilicho's Pictish War. *Britannia* VI, 141–5.

Pennington, W. (1970). Vegetation History in the North-West of England: a regional synthesis, in Walker D. and West, R. G. (eds.) *Studies in the Vegetational History of the British Isles*, pp. 41–79. Cambridge.

Potter, T. W. J. (1977). The Biglands Milefortlet and the Cumberland Coast Defences. *Britannia* VIII, 149–83.

Potter, T. W. J. (1979). *The Romans in North-West England*. Kendal.

Poulter, A. (1982). Old Penrith: Excavations 1977 and 1979. *CW²* 82, 51–66.

Richardson, A. (1982). Evidence for Centuriation in the Inglewood Forest. *CW²* 82, 67–71.

Richardson, G. G. S. (1977). A Romano–British Farmstead at Fingland. *CW²* 77, 53–9.

Richardson, G. G. S. and Richardson, A. (1980). A Possible Roman Road in the Kirkstone Pass and Matterdale. *CW²* 80, 160–2.

Richmond, I. A. (1933). Castlefolds by Great Asby. *CW²* 33, 233–7.

Richmond, I. A. (1935). The Rudge Cup: II. The Inscription. *Arch. Ael.* ⁴ 12, 334–42.

Richmond, I. A. (1936). Roman Leaden-Sealings from Brough-under-Stainmore. *CW²* 36, 104–25.

Richmond, I. A. (1945). The Sarmatae, Bremetenacum Veteranorum and the Regio Bremetennacensis. *JRS* 35, 15–29.

Richmond, I. A. (1951). A Roman Arterial Signalling System in the Stainmore Pass, in Grimes, W. F. (ed.) *Aspects of Archaeology in Britain and Beyond*, pp. 293–302. London.

Richmond, I. A. (1954). Queen Cartimandua. *JRS* 44, 43–52.

Richmond, I. A. and Crawford, O. G. S. (1949). The British Section of the Ravenna Cosmography. *Archaeologia* 93. 1–50.

Richmond, I. A. and McIntyre, J. (1934). The Roman Camps at Rey Cross and Crackenthorpe. *CW²* 34, 50–61.

Rivet, A. L. F. (1970). The British Section of the Antonine Itinerary. *Britannia* I, 34–82.

Robertson, A. S. (1973). The Antonine Wall. Glasgow.

St. Joseph, J. K. S. (1951). Air Reconnaissance of North Britain. *JRS* 41, 52–65.

Salway, P. (1980). The Vici: Urbanisation in the North, in Branigan, K. (ed.) *Rome and the Brigantes*, pp. 8–17. Sheffield.

Salway, P. (1981). *Roman Britain*. Oxford.

Shotter, D. C. A. (1973a). *Romans in Lancashire*. Clapham, Yorks.

Shotter, D. C. A. (1973b). Numeri Barcariorum: A Note on RIB 601. *Britannia* IV, 206–9.

Shotter, D. C. A. (1976). Coin Evidence and the Northern Frontier in the Second Century AD. *PSAS* 107, 81–91.

Shotter, D. C. A. (1978a). Roman Coins From Carlisle. *CW²* 78, 201–3.

Shotter, D. C. A. (1978b). Three Early Imperial Hoards from Lancashire. *Coin Hoards* 4, 44–5.

Shotter, D. C. A. (1979). The Evidence of Coin-Loss and the Roman Occupation of North-West England, in Higham, N. J. (ed.). *The Changing Past*, pp. 1–13. Manchester.

Shotter, D. C. A. (1980). Roman Coins from Starling Castle. *CW²* 80, 163.

Shotter, D. C. A. (1983). A Note on Tiles found on the Mitre Yard, Lancaster in 1973. *Britannia* XIV, 270–1.

Shotter, D. C. A. (1989). Roman Coin-finds in Cumbria. *CW²* 89, 41–50.

Shotter, D. C. A. (1990). *Roman Coins from North-West England*. Lancaster.

Shotter, D. C. A. and White, A. J. (1990). *The Roman Fort and Town of Lancaster*. Lancaster.

Simpson, F. G. and Hodgson, K. S. (1947). The Coastal Milefortlet at Cardurnock. *CW*2 47, 78–127.

Southworth, J. (1985). *Walking the Roman Roads in Cumbria*. Hale.

Start. D. (1985). Survey and Conservation Work at Castleshaw Roman Forts, 1984–5. *GMAJ* 1, 13–18.

Thompson, F. H. (1965). *Roman Cheshire*. Chester.

Thompson, F. H. (1976). The Excavation of the Roman Amphitheatre of Chester. *Archaeologia* 105, 127–239.

Thompson, F. H. (ed.) (1980). *Archaeology and Coastal Change*. London.

Tylecote, R. F. (1962). *Metallurgy in Archaeology*. London.

Walker, J. S. F. (1986). *Roman Manchester: A Frontier Settlement*. Manchester.

Ward, J. H. (1973). The British Sections of the Notitia Dignitatum: an alternative interpretation. *Britannia* IV, 253–63.

Webster, G. (1970). *The Roman Imperial Army*. London.

Webster, G. (1986). *The British Celts and Their Gods under Rome*. London.

Webster, P. V. (1975). The Later Roman Occupation at Wilderspool. *CAJ* 58, 91–2.

Wilkes, J. J. (1965). Early Fourth-Century Rebuilding in Hadrian's Wall Forts, in Jarrett, M. G. and Dobson, B. (eds.) *Britain and Rome*, pp. 114–38. Kendal.

Wooliscroft, D. J., (1988) The Outpost System of Hadrian's Wall. *CW*2 88, 23–8.

Wooliscroft, D. J. and Swain, S. A. M. (1991). The Roman 'Signal' Tower at Johnson's Plain. *CW*2 91, 19–29.

Occasional Papers from the Centre for North-West Regional Studies

Flowering Plants and Ferns of Cumbria	G. Halliday	£2.95
Early Lancaster Friends	M. Mullet	£2.95
North-West Theses and Dissertations, 1950–78	U. Lawler	£6.00
Lancaster: The Evolution of its Townscape to 1800	S. Penney	£2.95
Richard Marsden and the Preston Chartists, 1837–48	J. King	£2.95
The Grand Theatre, Lancaster	A. Betjemann	£2.95
Popular Leisure and the Music Hall in 19th-century Bolton	R. Poole	£2.95
Industrial Archaeology of the Lune Valley	J. Price	£2.95
The Diary of William Fisher of Barrow, 1811–59	W. Rollinson/B. Harrison	£2.95
Rural Life in South-West Lancashire, 1840–1914	A. Mutch	£3.95
Grand Fashionable Nights: Kendal Theatre, 1575–1985	M. Eddershaw	£3.95
The Roman Fort and Town of Lancaster	D. Shotter/A. White	£4.95
Windermere in the nineteenth century	O. M. Westall	£4.95
A Traditional Grocer: T. D. Smith's of Lancaster	M. Winstanley	£4.95
Reginald Farrer: Dalesman, Planthunter, Gardener	J. Illingworth/J. Routh	£4.95
Walking Roman Roads in Bowland	P. Graystone	£4.95
The Royal Albert: Chronicles of an Era	J. Alston	£4.95
From Lancaster to the Lakes – The Region in Literature	K. Hanley/A. Milbank	£5.95
The Buildings of Georgian Lancaster	A. White	£5.95
Lydia Becker and The Cause	A. Kelly	£5.95

Each of these titles may be ordered by post from:

C.N.W.R.S.,
Fylde College,
University of Lancaster,
Bailrigg, Lancaster

Books will be despatched post free to UK addresees.
Please make cheques payable to 'The University of Lancaster'.
Titles are also available from all good booksellers within the region.